INTERNET THEORY, TECHNOLOGY AND APPLICATIONS

TAXATION OF INTERNET SALES

INTERNET THEORY, TECHNOLOGY AND APPLICATIONS

Additional books in this series can be found on Nova's website
under the Series tab.

Additional e-books in this series can be found on Nova's website
under the e-books tab.

ECONOMIC ISSUES, PROBLEMS AND PERSPECTIVES

Additional books in this series can be found on Nova's website
under the Series tab.

Additional e-books in this series can be found on Nova's website
under the e-books tab.

INTERNET THEORY, TECHNOLOGY AND APPLICATIONS

TAXATION OF INTERNET SALES

KEITH JOYNER
AND
CARL SAWHILL
EDITORS

nova publishers

New York

For permission to use material from this book please contact us:
Telephone 631-231-7269; Fax 631-231-8175
Web Site: http://www.novapublishers.com

NOTICE TO THE READER

The Publisher has taken reasonable care in the preparation of this book, but makes no expressed or implied warranty of any kind and assumes no responsibility for any errors or omissions. No liability is assumed for incidental or consequential damages in connection with or arising out of information contained in this book. The Publisher shall not be liable for any special, consequential, or exemplary damages resulting, in whole or in part, from the readers' use of, or reliance upon, this material. Any parts of this book based on government reports are so indicated and copyright is claimed for those parts to the extent applicable to compilations of such works.

Independent verification should be sought for any data, advice or recommendations contained in this book. In addition, no responsibility is assumed by the publisher for any injury and/or damage to persons or property arising from any methods, products, instructions, ideas or otherwise contained in this publication.

This publication is designed to provide accurate and authoritative information with regard to the subject matter covered herein. It is sold with the clear understanding that the Publisher is not engaged in rendering legal or any other professional services. If legal or any other expert assistance is required, the services of a competent person should be sought. FROM A DECLARATION OF PARTICIPANTS JOINTLY ADOPTED BY A COMMITTEE OF THE AMERICAN BAR ASSOCIATION AND A COMMITTEE OF PUBLISHERS.

Additional color graphics may be available in the e-book version of this book.

Library of Congress Cataloging-in-Publication Data

ISBN: 978-1-62257-974-7

Published by Nova Science Publishers, Inc. ✝ *New York*

CONTENTS

PREFACE

As more and more purchases are made over the Internet, states are looking for new ways to collect taxes on these sales. While there is a common misperception that states cannot tax Internet sales, the reality is that they may impose sales and use taxes on such transactions, even when the retailer is outside of the state. However, if the seller does not have a constitutionally sufficient connection ("nexus") to the state, then the seller is under no enforceable obligation to collect a use tax. While the purchaser is still generally responsible for paying the use tax, the rate of compliance is low. Recent laws, often called "Amazon" laws in reference to the large Internet retailer, represent fresh attempts by the states to capture taxes on Internet sales. This book provides a constitutional analysis of "Amazon" laws and taxation of Internet sales; state taxation of Internet transations; and testimony on the hearing on the constitutional limitations on states' authority to collect sales taxes in E-commerce.

Chapter 1 – As more and more purchases are made over the Internet, states are looking for new ways to collect taxes on these sales. While there is a common misperception that states cannot tax Internet sales, the reality is that they may impose sales and use taxes on such transactions, even when the retailer is outside of the state. However, if the seller does not have a constitutionally sufficient connection ("nexus") to the state, then the seller is under no enforceable obligation to collect a use tax. While the purchaser is still generally responsible for paying the use tax, the rate of compliance is low. Recent laws, often called "Amazon" laws in reference to the large Internet retailer, represent fresh attempts by the states to capture taxes on Internet sales. States enacting these laws have used two basic approaches. The first is to impose use tax collection responsibilities on retailers who compensate state residents for placing links on the state residents' websites to the retailer's website (i.e., online referrals or "click-throughs"). The other is to require remote sellers to provide sales and tax-related information to the state and/or the in-state customers. New York was the first state to enact click-through legislation, and Colorado was the first to pass a notification law. These laws have received significant publicity, in part due to questions about whether they impermissibly impose duties on remote sellers who do not have a sufficient nexus to the state. Under Supreme Court jurisprudence, nexus is required by two provisions of the U.S. Constitution: the Due Process Clause of the Fourteenth Amendment and the Commerce Clause. The Court has held that, under the dormant Commerce Clause, a state may not impose tax collection responsibilities on an out-of-state seller that does not have a physical presence in the state. Importantly, physical presence is only required by the dormant Commerce Clause, which is subject to congressional regulation, while the Fourteenth Amendment imposes a lesser requirement. This means Congress may choose a different standard under its power to regulate interstate commerce, so long as such standard is consistent with due process. Legislation introduced in the 112th Congress—the Main Street Fairness Act (H.R. 2701 and S. 1452)—would authorize states to impose tax collection responsibilities on remote sellers once the act's requirements relating to state adoption of the multistate Streamlined Sales and Use Tax Agreement are met. The Marketplace Equity Act of 2011 (H.R. 3179), meanwhile, would allow a state to impose tax collection responsibilities on large remote sellers once it implemented a simplified tax administration system. The Marketplace Fairness Act (S. 1832) represents a hybrid approach in that it would allow a state to impose sales and use tax collection duties on remote sellers if the state were a member under the SSUTA or had adopted minimum simplification requirements, as provided under the act. Since Congress has not yet changed the physical presence standard under the Commerce Clause, it remains the standard by which to judge the constitutionality of the states' "Amazon" laws. Already, both the Colorado and New York laws have been challenged on constitutional grounds. The Colorado law, which applies mainly to companies without a physical presence in the state and imposes burdens on them not imposed on in-state retailers, appears to be the more constitutionally problematic approach, and it was recently struck down by a federal district court. A state appellate court in New York, meanwhile, has rejected a claim that the New York law violates both clauses on its face, but has kept alive an as-applied challenge. The constitutionality of the New York law appears to primarily turn on whether state residents can be characterized as engaging in a constitutionally significant level of solicitation on behalf of the Internet retailer so that it can be treated as having a physical presence in the state. Recently, several states have enacted legislation intended to capture use taxes on sales made by out-of-state sellers to in-state customers. These laws are commonly referred to as "Amazon" laws, in reference to the large Internet retailer. A use tax is the companion to a sales tax—the sales tax is imposed on the sale of goods and services within the state's borders, while the use tax is imposed on purchases made by the state's residents from out-of-state (remote) sellers. The purpose of the use tax is to dissuade residents from purchasing goods and services from out-of-state merchants in order to avoid the sales tax. Two common misconceptions exist about the ability of states to impose sales and use taxes on Internet sales. The first is that the Internet Tax Freedom Act, enacted in 1998, prevents such taxation. This is not the case. The act contains a moratorium only on state and local governments imposing "multiple or discriminatory taxes on electronic commerce," as well as new taxes on Internet access services. As a result of this law, a state may not, for example, impose a tax on electronic commerce that is not imposed on similar transactions made through other means (such as traditional "brick and mortar" stores). It remains permissible, however, for a state to impose a sales or use tax that is administered equally without regard to whether the sale was face-to-face, mail order, or Internet. The second misperception is that the U.S. Constitution prohibits states from taxing Internet sales. States have the power to tax their residents, even when the seller is located outside of the state and has no real connection with the state. What the Constitution restricts is the state's ability to require an out-of-state seller to collect the use tax. While the purchaser is still generally responsible for paying the use tax, the rate of purchaser compliance is low. Thus, states have been motivated to develop new ways in which they can capture the use taxes that are going uncollected on Internet sales. This recent state activity and the constitutional limitations on it are the focus of this report.

Chapter 2 – The United States Bureau of the Census estimated that $3.4 trillion worth of retail and wholesale transactions were conducted over the Internet in 2009. That amount was 16.8% of all U.S. shipments and sales in that year. Other estimates projected the 2011 so-called e-commerce volume at approximately $3.9 trillion. The volume of e-commerce is expected to increase and state and local governments are concerned because collection of sales taxes on these transactions is difficult to enforce. Under current law, states cannot reach beyond their borders and compel out-of-state Internet vendors (those without nexus in the buyer's state) to collect the use tax owed by state residents and businesses. The Supreme Court ruled in 1967 that requiring remote vendors to collect the use tax would pose an undue burden on interstate commerce. Estimates put this lost tax revenue at approximately $11.4 billion in 2012. Congress is involved because interstate commerce typically falls under the Commerce Clause of the Constitution. Opponents of remote vendor sales and use tax collection cite the complexity of the myriad state and local sales tax systems and the difficulty vendors would have in collecting and remitting use taxes. Proponents would like Congress to change the law and allow states to require out-of-state vendors without nexus to collect state use taxes. These proponents acknowledge that simplification and harmonization of state tax systems are likely prerequisites for Congress to consider approval of increased collection authority for states. A number of states have been working together to harmonize sales tax collection and have created the Streamlined Sales and Use Tax Agreement (SSUTA). The SSUTA member states hope that Congress can be persuaded to allow them to require out-of-state vendors to collect taxes from customers in SSUTA member states. In the 112th Congress, S. 1452 and H.R. 2701 (Senator Durbin and Representative Conyers) would grant SSUTA member states the authority to compel out-of-state vendors in other member states to collect sales and use taxes. In addition, H.R. 3179 (Representative Womack) would also grant states the authority to compel out-of-state vendors to collect use taxes provided selected simplification efforts are implemented. S. 1832 (Senator Enzi and others including Senator Durbin) would grant SSUTA member states and non-member states that meet less rigorous simplifications standards the authority to compel out-of-state vendors to collect sales and use taxes. A related issue is the "Internet Tax Moratorium." The relatively narrow moratorium prohibits (1) new taxes on Internet access services and (2) multiple or discriminatory taxes on Internet commerce. Congress has extended the "Internet Tax Moratorium" twice. The most recent extension expires November 1, 2014. The moratorium is distinct from the remote use tax collection issue, but has been linked in past debates. An analysis of the Internet tax moratorium is beyond the scope of this report.

Chapter 3 – Statement of House Judiciary Committee Chairman Lamar Smith.

Chapter 4 – Testimony of Dan Marshall, Owner, Marshall Music Co.

Chapter 5 – Testimony of Dr. Patrick M. Byrne, Chairman and CEO, Overstock.com, Inc.

Chapter 6 – Testimony of John Otto, Representative, Texas House of Representatives.

Chapter 7 – Testimony of Tod Cohen, Vice President and Deputy General Counsel, eBay, Inc.

Chapter 8 – Testimony of Senator Howard Kenley III, Indiana Senate.

Chapter 9 – Testimony of Paul Misener, Vice President for Global Public Policy, Amazon.com.

Chapter 10 – Statement of Congresswoman Jackie Speier.

Chapter 11 – Statement of Hanns Kuttner, Visiting Fellow, Hudson Institute.

Chapter 12 – Statement of Steve DelBianco, Executive Director, NetChoice.

Chapter 13 – Statement of Joseph Henchman, Vice President, Tax Foundation.

In: Taxation of Internet Sales   ISBN: 978-1-62257-974-7
Editors: Keith Joyner and Carl Sawhill   © 2013 Nova Science Publishers, Inc.

Chapter 1

"AMAZON" LAWS AND TAXATION OF INTERNET SALES: CONSTITUTIONAL ANALYSIS[*]

Erika K. Lunder and John R. Luckey

SUMMARY

As more and more purchases are made over the Internet, states are looking for new ways to collect taxes on these sales. While there is a common misperception that states cannot tax Internet sales, the reality is that they may impose sales and use taxes on such transactions, even when the retailer is outside of the state. However, if the seller does not have a constitutionally sufficient connection ("nexus") to the state, then the seller is under no enforceable obligation to collect a use tax. While the purchaser is still generally responsible for paying the use tax, the rate of compliance is low.

Recent laws, often called "Amazon" laws in reference to the large Internet retailer, represent fresh attempts by the states to capture taxes on Internet sales. States enacting these laws have used two basic approaches. The first is to impose use tax collection responsibilities on retailers who compensate state residents for placing links on the state residents' websites to the retailer's website (i.e., online referrals or "click-throughs"). The other is to require

---

[*] This is an edited, reformatted and augmented version of the Congressional Research Service Publication, CRS Report for Congress R42629, dated July 26, 2012.

remote sellers to provide sales and tax-related information to the state and/or the in-state customers. New York was the first state to enact click-through legislation, and Colorado was the first to pass a notification law. These laws have received significant publicity, in part due to questions about whether they impermissibly impose duties on remote sellers who do not have a sufficient nexus to the state.

Under Supreme Court jurisprudence, nexus is required by two provisions of the U.S. Constitution: the Due Process Clause of the Fourteenth Amendment and the Commerce Clause. The Court has held that, under the dormant Commerce Clause, a state may not impose tax collection responsibilities on an out-of-state seller that does not have a physical presence in the state. Importantly, physical presence is only required by the dormant Commerce Clause, which is subject to congressional regulation, while the Fourteenth Amendment imposes a lesser requirement. This means Congress may choose a different standard under its power to regulate interstate commerce, so long as such standard is consistent with due process. Legislation introduced in the 112th Congress—the Main Street Fairness Act (H.R. 2701 and S. 1452)—would authorize states to impose tax collection responsibilities on remote sellers once the act's requirements relating to state adoption of the multistate Streamlined Sales and Use Tax Agreement are met. The Marketplace Equity Act of 2011 (H.R. 3179), meanwhile, would allow a state to impose tax collection responsibilities on large remote sellers once it implemented a simplified tax administration system. The Marketplace Fairness Act (S. 1832) represents a hybrid approach in that it would allow a state to impose sales and use tax collection duties on remote sellers if the state were a member under the SSUTA or had adopted minimum simplification requirements, as provided under the act.

Since Congress has not yet changed the physical presence standard under the Commerce Clause, it remains the standard by which to judge the constitutionality of the states' "Amazon" laws. Already, both the Colorado and New York laws have been challenged on constitutional grounds. The Colorado law, which applies mainly to companies without a physical presence in the state and imposes burdens on them not imposed on in-state retailers, appears to be the more constitutionally problematic approach, and it was recently struck down by a federal district court. A state appellate court in New York, meanwhile, has rejected a claim that the New York law violates both clauses on its face, but has kept alive an as-applied challenge. The constitutionality of the New York law appears to primarily turn on whether state residents can be characterized as engaging in a constitutionally significant level of solicitation on behalf of the Internet retailer so that it can be treated as having a physical presence in the state.

Recently, several states have enacted legislation intended to capture use taxes on sales made by out-of-state sellers to in-state customers. These laws are commonly referred to as "Amazon" laws, in reference to the large Internet retailer.

A use tax is the companion to a sales tax—the sales tax is imposed on the sale of goods and services within the state's borders, while the use tax is imposed on purchases made by the state's residents from out-of-state (remote) sellers.[1] The purpose of the use tax is to dissuade residents from purchasing goods and services from out-of-state merchants in order to avoid the sales tax.[2]

Two common misconceptions exist about the ability of states to impose sales and use taxes on Internet sales. The first is that the Internet Tax Freedom Act, enacted in 1998, prevents such taxation.[3] This is not the case. The act contains a moratorium[4] only on state and local governments imposing "multiple or discriminatory taxes on electronic commerce," as well as new taxes on Internet access services. As a result of this law, a state may not, for example, impose a tax on electronic commerce that is not imposed on similar transactions made through other means (such as traditional "brick and mortar" stores).[5] It remains permissible, however, for a state to impose a sales or use tax that is administered equally without regard to whether the sale was face-to-face, mail order, or Internet.[6]

The second misperception is that the U.S. Constitution prohibits states from taxing Internet sales. States have the power to tax their residents, even when the seller is located outside of the state and has no real connection with the state. What the Constitution restricts is the state's ability to require an out-of-state seller to collect the use tax. While the purchaser is still generally responsible for paying the use tax, the rate of purchaser compliance is low. Thus, states have been motivated to develop new ways in which they can capture the use taxes that are going uncollected on Internet sales. This recent state activity and the constitutional limitations on it are the focus of this report.

CONSTITUTIONAL REQUIREMENTS

As discussed below under "Recent State Legislation," several states have enacted legislation aimed at collecting taxes from Internet sales by imposing tax collection or notification requirements on Internet retailers. These laws potentially implicate two provisions of the U.S. Constitution: the Fourteenth Amendment's Due Process Clause[7] and the dormant Commerce Clause.[8] The clauses have different purposes, and a state's imposition of tax liability on a retailer may be acceptable under one and not the other.[9] The concern under the Due Process Clause is whether imposition of the liability is fair; while the concern under the dormant Commerce Clause is whether it unduly burdens interstate commerce. Together, these clauses impose two requirements relevant for analyzing the states' "Amazon" laws: (1) both require there be some type of nexus between the state and remote vendor before the state can impose the liability; and (2) the dormant Commerce Clause prohibits states from discriminating against out-of-state sellers. An important point to emphasize at the outset is that Congress has the authority under its commerce power to permit state taxation that would otherwise violate the dormant Commerce Clause.[10]

Nexus

In order for a state to impose tax liability on an out-of-state business, a constitutionally sufficient connection or "nexus" must exist between the state and business. Nexus is required by both the Due Process Clause and the dormant Commerce Clause. Due process requires there be a sufficient nexus between the state and seller so that the state has provided some benefit for which it may ask something in return and the seller has fair warning that its activities may be subject to the state's jurisdiction.[11] The dormant Commerce Clause, meanwhile, requires a nexus in order to ensure that the state's imposition of the liability does not impermissibly burden interstate commerce.[12]

The nexus standard is not the same under both clauses. The Supreme Court has ruled that, absent congressional action, the standard required under the dormant Commerce Clause is the seller's physical presence in the state,[13] while due process imposes a lesser standard under which the seller must have directed purposeful contact at the state's residents.[14]

This was not always the case. The first time the Court articulated the physical presence requirement, in the 1967 decision *National Bellas Hess v. Dept. of Revenue of Illinois*,[15] it grounded the requirement in both the Due Process and Commerce Clauses. The Court noted that each required a similar connection between the state and seller liable for the tax: due process required that "the state has given anything for which it can ask return," while state taxes on interstate commercial transactions were permissible when they represented "a fair share of the cost of the local government whose protection [the seller] enjoys."[16] The Court held these requirements meant that a state's authority to impose tax collection responsibility was limited to when the merchant had a physical presence in the state.[17] The Court also noted that due to the significant number of taxing jurisdictions across the country and the complexity of their administrative and collection requirements, the imposition of the tax liability would create an unacceptable burden on interstate commerce.[18]

By the late 1980s, it seemed possible that physical presence was no longer the rule because the Court had modified its analysis of both the Due Process and Commerce Clauses. First, due process was no longer interpreted to require an individual or entity's physical presence in a state before a state could exercise authority over the individual or entity; instead, liability could be imposed when the individual or entity intentionally made a sufficient level of contact with the state.[19] Second, the Court, rather than enforcing bright-line prohibitions against certain types of taxation on interstate commerce, developed a test to determine whether a tax placed an unacceptable burden on interstate commerce.[20] Since one reason the use tax responsibility was unconstitutional was due to its burdensomeness, it was possible that technological advances had reduced the complexity of collecting the taxes to an acceptable level under the new test.

However, in the 1992 case *Quill v. North Dakota*,[21] the Supreme Court rejected the idea that physical presence was no longer required and held that a state could still not impose use tax collection liability under the dormant Commerce Clause on a mail-order seller without a physical presence in the state, absent congressional action. While the Court affirmed the holding in *Bellas Hess*, it did not entirely adopt the same rationale. As in *Bellas Hess*, the Court found that collecting the tax would be an impermissible burden on interstate commerce, absent congressional action, and again noted the magnitude of the potential burden of such tax in light of the numerous taxing jurisdictions across the country.[22] The Court, however, altered its reasoning from *Bellas Hess* by expressly rejecting the idea that *due process* requires physical presence. The Court, noting that the two clauses served different purposes, found that its due process analysis had evolved so that physical presence was not necessary so long as the seller had directed some actions at the state's residents.[23] The Court found such purposeful contact existed in *Quill* since the seller had "continuous and widespread solicitation of business" within the state.[24]

The Supreme Court has not revisited the issue since *Quill*. Nonetheless, several pre-*Quill* cases provide guidance on determining when a state may impose tax collection responsibilities on out-of-state retailers. Clearly, a state can impose such responsibilities on a company with a "brick and mortar" retail store or offices in the state.[25] This seems to be the case even if the in-state offices and the sales giving rise to the tax liability are unrelated to one another. For example, the Court has held that a state could require a company to collect use taxes on mail order sales to in-state customers when the company maintained two offices in the state that generated significant revenue, even though the offices were used to sell advertising space in the company's magazine and had nothing to do with the company's mail-order business.[26] The Court firmly rejected the argument that there needed to be a nexus not only between the company and the state, but also between the state and the sales activity. It reasoned that there was a sufficient connection between the state and company as the two in-state offices had enjoyed the "advantage of the same municipal services" whether or not they were connected to the mail-order business.[27]

Absent some type of physical office or retail space in the state, it also seems that having in-state salespeople or agents is sufficient contact. In several cases pre-dating *Bellas Hess* and *Quill*, the Court upheld the power of the state to impose use tax collection liabilities on remote sellers when the sales were arranged by local agents or salespeople.[28] For example, in one of these cases, *Scripto, Inc. v. Carson*,[29] which the Court later described as "represent[ing] the furthest constitutional reach to date" of a state's ability to impose use tax collection duties on a remote seller,[30] the Court held that a state could impose use tax collection liability on an out-of-state company that had no presence in the state other than 10 "independent contractors" who solicited business for the company. These individuals had limited power in that they had no authority to make collections or incur debts on behalf of the company and merely forwarded the orders they solicited to the company's out-of-state headquarters, where the decision to fill the order was made. Nonetheless, the Court held that there was a constitutionally sufficient nexus between the company and the state because the individuals had conducted "continuous local solicitation" in the state on behalf of the company.[31] The Court also noted that their status as independent contractors instead of regular employees was constitutionally insignificant.[32]

Discriminatory Taxes

The Commerce Clause also prohibits state laws that discriminate against interstate commerce.[33] A state law that "regulates even-handedly to effectuate a legitimate local public interest" and has "only incidental" effect on interstate commerce is constitutionally permissible "unless the burden imposed on such commerce is clearly excessive in relation to the putative local benefits."[34] On the other hand, a facially discriminatory state law is "virtually *per se* invalid."[35] Traditionally, such laws have only been permissible if they meet the high standard of "advanc[ing] a legitimate local purpose that cannot be adequately served by reasonable nondiscriminatory alternatives."[36] Thus, a state law that subjected remote sellers to tax-related burdens not imposed on in-state sellers would appear to be facially discriminatory and, therefore, subject to a high level of judicial scrutiny.

CONGRESSIONAL AUTHORITY TO ACT

The fact that the Supreme Court in *Quill* separated the nexus analysis under the Due Process Clause from that under the dormant Commerce Clause has important ramifications for Congress. Under its authority to regulate commerce, Congress has the power to authorize state action that would otherwise be an unconstitutional burden on interstate commerce, so long as it is consistent with other provisions in the Constitution.[37] When the Court held in *Bellas Hess* that both the Due Process and Commerce Clauses required physical presence, Congress could not have used its commerce power to impose a lesser standard because the Fourteenth Amendment still required physical presence. Since the Court in *Quill* found that the nexus standard for due process was less than that required by the dormant Commerce Clause, this means Congress can permit state taxation without physical presence, assuming the minimum connection necessary to satisfy the Due Process Clause is met.[38]

Congress has thus far not defined the nexus standard, although legislation to do so has been introduced in the 112th Congress: the Main Street Fairness Act (H.R. 2701 and S. 1452), the Marketplace Equity Act of 2011 (H.R. 3179), and the Marketplace Fairness Act (S. 1832). As with previous legislation,[39] the Main Street Fairness Act is linked to the Streamlined Sales Tax Project. The project was formed by state tax administrators in 2000 in order to simplify and make uniform the administration of sales and use taxes among the states.[40] In 2002, member states adopted the Streamlined Sales and

Use Tax Agreement (SSUTA),[41] and efforts are now aimed at each state's adoption of changes to its taxing scheme in order to come into compliance with the agreement. According to the project's website, 44 states and the District of Columbia participate in the project, and 24 states have enacted conforming legislation.[42]

The Main Street Fairness Act would authorize each SSUTA member state to impose sales and use tax collection responsibilities on remote sellers (other than small sellers) for sales sourced to that state under the agreement. The authorization would come into effect once 10 states comprising at least 20% of the population of all states with a sales tax have become members under the SSUTA; various operational aspects of the agreement have been implemented; and each member state has met requirements relating to databases and taxability matrices. Additionally, the SSUTA would be required to meet specified minimum simplification requirements (e.g., multistate registration system; uniform definitions and rules for sourcing; single state-level administration of state and local sales and use taxes). It appears at least one of the criteria—the population requirement—has been met.[43]

The Marketplace Equity Act of 2011, meanwhile, would authorize a state to impose tax collection responsibilities on large remote sellers once it implemented a simplified tax administration system. The state's sales and use tax system would have to meet minimum requirements relating to streamlined return filing; uniform tax base and exemptions throughout the state; and the sales and use tax rate structure. A state meeting the requirements could begin to require remote sellers to collect the taxes on the first day of the calendar year that was at least six months after the state published a public notice regarding the collection responsibilities. That notice would have to include information relating to the state law requiring remote sellers to collect the taxes; the criteria under which the taxes must be collected; the tax rate(s); the date taxes must start being collected; and tax return filing and compliance.

Finally, the Marketplace Fairness Act represents a hybrid approach. It would authorize states to impose sales and use tax collection responsibilities on sales sourced to that state if the state had adopted the SSUTA or implemented minimum simplification requirements, as provided in the act. As with the other bills, exceptions would exist for small sellers.

RECENT STATE LEGISLATION

Facing the ongoing economic recession, many states have considered legislation designed to raise revenue by increasing the collection of use taxes from Internet sales. Two primary approaches have developed: "click-through nexus" and notification requirements. This section examines these approaches by focusing on the laws in the first states to enact legislation: New York's click-through nexus statute and Colorado's required notification law.

Click-through Nexus

One approach adopted by some states is "click-through nexus." This term arises from the "clickthroughs"—online referrals—that Internet retailers solicit through efforts such as Amazon's "Amazon Associates" program.[44] In this type of program, an individual or business that operates a website places a link on that website that directs Internet users to a different website that offers products or services from an online retailer such as Amazon. In Amazon's program, these "associate" individuals or businesses receive, as compensation for their referral, a percentage of the income Amazon realizes when an Internet user "clicks through" from one of these links and purchases Amazon goods and services.

"Click-through nexus" statutes require an online retailer to collect use taxes on sales to customers located in the taxing state based on the physical presence in that state of the retailer's "associates." An example of such a law is the one enacted by New York in 2008.

Under New York law, vendors are required to collect sales and use taxes, with vendors defined to include any entity which "solicits business" through "employees, independent contractors, agents or other representatives."[45] The 2008 law added a statutory presumption that sellers of taxable property and services meet this requirement:

> if the seller enters into an agreement with a resident of this state under which the resident, for a commission or other consideration, directly or indirectly refers potential customers, whether by a link on an Internet website or otherwise, to the seller.[46]

According to guidance issued by the state's tax agency, the presumption is not triggered by placing an advertisement.[47] For these purposes, advertising does not include placing a direct or indirect link to the seller's website if the consideration for such placement is based on the sales generated by the link.[48] Finally, the presumption may be rebutted by proof that the resident "did not engage in any solicitation in the state on behalf of the seller that would satisfy the [Constitution's] nexus requirement" during the preceding four sales and use tax quarterly periods.[49]

New York's statute tries to capture more remote sellers in the gap between those that fall within the *Bellas Hess/Quill* safe harbor, who clearly cannot be compelled to collect use taxes, and those that maintain property or direct employees in the taxing state, which Amazon and other Internet retailers have taken great care not to do. On the one hand, it might be argued that the law complies with the Supreme Court's jurisprudence by targeting only Internet retailers whose "affiliate" programs create some degree of physical presence in the state and whose "affiliates" solicit (i.e., do more than merely advertise) on the retailer's behalf. Examined in this light, the law might be characterized as similar to the one at issue in *Scripto*, where the Court upheld the power of the state to require use tax collection by a remote seller whose sales were arranged by local "independent contractors" who forwarded the orders they solicited to the company's out-of-state headquarters.[50] In that case, the Court made clear that the individuals' title was unimportant, as was the fact that they had no authority over the sales (e.g., could not approve them).[51] Rather, the key factor in the Court's decision was that the individuals had conducted "continuous local solicitation" in the state on behalf of the company.[52] By targeting those affiliates which solicit in the state, it seems the argument could be made that the New York law is within the Court's *Scripto* holding and, therefore, is constitutional with respect to affiliates with sufficient solicitation activities.

On the other hand, it might be argued there is reason to question whether linking on a website is substantively similar to the "continuous local solicitation" conducted by the salespeople in *Scripto*. It might be argued that the *Scripto* salespeople's on-going activities are distinguishable from the one-time action of placing a link on a website. A court examining whether this difference is constitutionally significant might be particularly hesitant about extending *Scripto's* holding since the *Bellas Hess* Court referred to it as "represent[ing] the furthest constitutional reach to date" of a state's ability to require use tax collection by a remote seller.[53] Another question may be whether a court would find the New York law to be unconstitutionally burdensome by requiring remote sellers to potentially monitor thousands of affiliates in order to determine whether the nexus requirement has been met.[54]

Whether New York's strategy of taxing Internet retailers based on the presence in the taxing state of "affiliates" or "associates" will survive constitutional scrutiny and prove to be the "Holy Grail of remote taxation,"[55] as some have called it, remains to be seen. Amazon has filed suit in New York state court, alleging facial and as-applied invalidity under, among other things, the Commerce Clause and Due Process Clause. The company argues that the Supreme Court's jurisprudence stands only for the proposition that substantial nexus can be created by "active solicitation" in the taxing state on behalf of an out-of-state retailer, a standard which "click-through" referrals do not meet.[56] After the trial court dismissed the case,[57] the state appellate court rejected the facial challenges under both clauses, but remanded the case with respect to the claim of as-applied invalidity under both clauses.[58] When rejecting the facial challenge under the Commerce Clause, the appellate court found "the nexus requirement is satisfied" because the law imposes tax collection responsibility on remote vendors "only where the vendor enters into a business-referral agreement with a New York State resident, and only when that resident receives a commission based on a sale in New York" and "does not target the out-of-state vendor's sales through agents who are not New York residents."[59] With respect to the facial due process challenge, the appellate court rejected the claims that the law's presumption was irrational and irrebuttable and that the law was unconstitutionally vague.[60]

Required Notification

The second approach adopted by some states requires Internet retailers to provide information to the state and/or customer, rather than requiring Internet retailers to collect the use taxes themselves. This approach is illustrated by Colorado's law, which was enacted in 2010.

Among other things, Colorado's law imposes three duties on any "retailer that does not collect Colorado sales tax."[61] Retailers must (1) inform Colorado customers that a sales or use tax is owed on certain purchases and that it is the customer's responsibility to file a tax return; (2) send each Colorado customer a year-end notice of the date, amount, and category of each purchase made during the previous year, as well as a reminder that the state requires taxes be paid and returns filed for certain purchases; and (3) provide an annual statement to the Colorado department of revenue for each in-state customer showing the total amount paid for purchases during the year. Unless the retailer can show reasonable cause, each failure to notify a customer about the duty to file a state use tax return carries a $5 penalty, while each failure of the other two duties carries a $10 penalty.[62]

The notification requirements apply only to companies that do not collect Colorado sales and use taxes, which would appear to be primarily those retailers without a substantial nexus to the state. In other words, the law applies to companies that do not have a physical presence in the state. The first question is whether this violates due process. While the law targets companies without physical presence in the state, it applies to "retailers" who, by definition, must be "doing business" in the state.[63] This means the notification law applies only to retailers who have some type of contact with the state. However, there may be retailers for whom the "doing business" standard would not result in the requisite minimum connection with the state.

Additionally, the Colorado statute raises two issues under the Commerce Clause. First, since the law applies to companies that do not have a physical presence in the state, it would appear that the notification requirements would have to be distinguishable from use tax collection responsibilities in order to be permissible. On the one hand, some might distinguish between them since the notification law does not actually impose any tax collection liability on remote sellers, unlike the laws at issue in *Bellas Hess* and *Quill*. On the other hand, some might characterize the laws as functionally similar since all are intended to increase use tax collection, in which case it might be argued that the notification requirements are at least as burdensome as tax collection responsibilities since both require similar types of recordkeeping and, unlike collection responsibilities, the notification law also involves reporting information to the consumer. A court adopting this characterization of the notification duties would likely find them to be an impermissible burden on interstate commerce.

Second, by targeting remote sellers that do not have a physical presence in the state, the law imposes duties on out-of-state business that are not similarly imposed on Colorado businesses. Thus, it appears to be a facially discriminatory law. Under the Supreme Court's jurisprudence, facially discriminatory laws are "virtually *per se* invalid."[64] In order to be upheld against constitutional challenge, they generally must meet the high standard of "advanc[ing] a legitimate local purpose that cannot be adequately served by reasonable nondiscriminatory alternatives."[65] Whether the Colorado law would meet this high standard is open to question. While collecting use tax on purchases made to in-state customers seems an obvious legitimate government purpose, some might argue that there are other alternatives, such as collecting use tax from state residents on the state income tax form.

The constitutionality of the Colorado law has already been challenged. In March 2012, a federal district court held that the law violates the dormant Commerce Clause.[66] First, the Court found that the state law impermissibly discriminated against out-of-state vendors. The court explained the only way a discriminatory law could be saved was if the state were able to show that its legitimate interests could not be served by reasonable nondiscriminatory alternatives, which the court found the state had completely failed to do.[67] Second, the court found the notification requirements were "inextricably related in kind and purpose" to the tax collection responsibilities at issue in *Quill* and therefore subject to the physical presence standard.[68] Since the Colorado requirements applied to retailers without a physical presence in the state, the court concluded they were in violation of the protections established by *Quill* and therefore unconstitutional.[69]

End Notes

[1] For information on state sales and use taxes, see CRS Report R41853, *State Taxation of Internet Transactions*, by Steven Maguire.

[2] *See* Miller Bros. Co. v. Maryland, 347 U.S 340, 343 (1954)("The use tax, not in itself a relatively significant revenue producer, usually appears as a support to the sales tax in two respects. One is protection of the state's revenues by taking away from inhabitants the advantages of resort to untaxed out-of-state purchases. The other is protection of local merchants against out-of-state competition from those who may be enabled by lower tax burdens to offer lower prices.").

[3] P.L. 105-277, Div. C, Title XI, 112 Stat. 2681-719, *found at* 47 U.S.C. §151 note (hereinafter *Internet Tax Freedom Act*). For more information on the act, see CRS Report RL33261, *Internet Taxation: Issues and Legislation*, by Steven Maguire and Nonna A. Noto.

[4] The moratorium, which was originally set to expire in 2001, has been extended several times and is now in effect until November 1, 2014. P.L. 107-75, §2, 115 Stat. 703 (the Internet Tax Nondiscrimination Act of 2001 extended the moratorium through November 1, 2003); P.L. 108-435, §§2, 8, 118 Stat. 2615 (the Internet Tax Nondiscrimination Act extended the moratorium retroactively from November 1, 2003, to November 1, 2007); P.L. 110-108, §2, 121 Stat. 1024 (the Internet Tax Freedom Act Amendments Act of 2007 extended the moratorium to November 1, 2014).

[5] *See Internet Tax Freedom Act*, *supra* note 3, at §1105(2) (definition of "discriminatory tax").

[6] *See id.* at §1101(b) ("Except as provided in this section [imposing the moratorium] nothing in this title shall be construed to modify, impair, or supersede, or authorize the modification, impairment, or superseding of, any State or local law pertaining to taxation that is otherwise permissible by or under the Constitution of the United States or other Federal law and in effect on the date of enactment of this Act.").

[7] U.S. CONST. Amend. 14, §1 ("nor shall any State deprive any person of life, liberty, or property, without due process of law ... ").

[8] U.S. CONST. art. 1 §8, cl.3 ("The Congress shall have Power ... To regulate Commerce with foreign Nations, and among the several States, and with the Indian Tribes."). The Supreme Court has long held that because the Constitution grants Congress the authority to regulate interstate commerce, the states may not unduly burden such commerce—this is known as

the dormant, or negative, Commerce Clause. *See* Okla. Tax Comm'n v. Jefferson Lines, 514 U.S. 175, 180 (1995) (dormant Commerce Clause "reflect[s] a central concern of the Framers" that "the new Union would have to avoid the tendencies toward economic Balkanization that had plagued relations among the Colonies and later among the States under the Articles of Confederation.") The dormant Commerce Clause "prevent[s] a State from retreating into economic isolation or jeopardizing the welfare of the Nation as a whole, as it would do if it were free to place burdens on the flow of commerce across its borders that commerce wholly within those borders would not bear." *Id.*; Southern Pacific Co. v. Arizona, 325 U.S. 761, 768 (1945)(further rationale is that out-of-state entities subject to any burden are likely not in a position to use the state's political process to seek relief).

[9] *See* Quill v. North Dakota, 504 U.S. 298, 312 (1992).

[10] *See id.* at 318 ("[O]ur decision is made easier by the fact that the underlying issue is not only one that Congress may be better qualified to resolve, but also one that Congress has the ultimate power to resolve. No matter how we evaluate the burdens that use taxes impose on interstate commerce, Congress remains free to disagree with our conclusions ... Accordingly, Congress is now free to decide whether, when, and to what extent the States may burden interstate mail-order concerns with a duty to collect use taxes.").

[11] *See id.* at 308.

[12] *See* Complete Auto Transit, Inc. v Brady, 430 U.S. 274 (1977).

[13] *See* National Bellas Hess Inc. v. Dep't. of Rev. of Illinois, 386 U.S. 753 (1967); *Quill*, 504 U.S. at 317-18.

[14] *See Quill*, 504 U.S. at 308.

[15] National Bellas Hess v. Dep't. of Revenue of Illinois, 386 U.S. 753 (1967); *see also* Miller Bros. Co. v. Maryland, 347 U.S. 340, 347 (1954) (finding insufficient nexus, based solely on due process grounds, when the seller's activities did not involve the "invasion or exploitation of the consumer market in" the taxing state, with the Court contrasting "active and aggressive operation within a taxing state" with the seller's "occasional delivery of goods sold at an out-of-state store with no solicitation other than the incidental effects of general advertising").

[16] *Bellas Hess*, 386 U.S. at 756.

[17] *Id.* at 758.

[18] *Id.* at 759-60.

[19] Many of these cases addressed whether an individual or entity could be subject to suit in a state court. For example, in *Burger King v. Rudzewicz*, 471 U.S. 462 (1985), the Court held that a Michigan franchisee without any contacts to Florida could be subject to suit in Florida court after entering into a contract with a Florida corporation. The Court wrote, "So long as a commercial actor's efforts are 'purposefully directed' towards residents of another State, we have consistently rejected the notion that an absence of physical contacts can defeat personal jurisdiction there [citations omitted]." *Id.* at 476.

[20] *See* Complete Auto Transit, Inc. v. Brady, 430 U.S. 274 (1977).

[21] Quill v. North Dakota, 504 U.S. 298 (1992).

[22] *Id.* at 313.

[23] *See id.* at 308.

[24] *Id.* ("In 'modern commercial life' it matters little that such solicitation is accomplished by a deluge of catalogs rather than a phalanx of drummers: The requirements of due process are met irrespective of a corporation's lack of physical presence in the taxing State.").

[25] *See* Nelson v. Sears, Roebuck & Co., 312 U.S. 359 (1941)(upholding imposition of state use tax collection liability on mail order sales when company had retail stores in the state); Nelson v. Montgomery Ward, 312 U.S. 373 (1941) (same); *see also* D.H. Holmes Co., Ltd. v. McNamara, 486 U.S. 24, 32-33 (1988)(upholding imposition of use tax on company with 13 stores in the state).

[26] Nat'l Geographic Soc. v. California Bd. of Equalization, 430 U.S. 551 (1977).

[27] *Id.* at 561.

[28] *See* Scripto, Inc. v. Carson, 362 U.S. 207, 211 (1960)(discussed *infra*); Felt & Tarrant Co. v. Gallagher, 306 U.S. 62 (1939) (upholding state imposition of use tax collection liability on company with two agents in the state); General Trading Co. v. Tax Comm'n, 322 U.S. 335 (1944) (upholding state imposition of use tax collection liability on company with salespeople in the state).

[29] Scripto, Inc. v. Carson, 362 U.S. 207 (1960).

[30] *Bellas Hess*, 386 U.S. at 757.

[31] *Id.* at 211.

[32] *See id.*

[33] *See* Complete Auto Transit, Inc. v. Brady, 430 U.S. 274, 279 (1977); *see also* Oregon Waste Systems, Inc. v. Dep't of Environmental Quality, 511 U.S. 93, 98 (1994)(dormant Commerce Clause "denies the States the power unjustifiably to discriminate against or burden the interstate flow of articles of commerce").

[34] Pike v. Bruce Church, Inc., 397 U.S. 137, 142 (1970).

[35] Camps Newfound/Owatonna, Inc. v. Town of Harrison, 520 U.S. 564, 575 (1997) (internal citations omitted); *see also* Hughes v. Oklahoma, 441 U.S. 322, 336 (1979).

[36] New Energy Co. of Indiana v. Limbach, 486 U.S. 269, 278 (1988); *see also* Hughes v. Oklahoma, 441 U.S. 322, 336-37 (1979)(imposing same test).

[37] *See* Northeast Bancorp v. Board of Governors of Fed. Reserve Sys., 472 U.S. 159, 174 (1985)("state actions [that burden interstate commerce] which [Congress] plainly authorizes are invulnerable to constitutional attack under the Commerce Clause. [citations omitted]"); *see also* Prudential Insurance Co. v. Benjamin, 328 U.S. 408, 434 (1946)(describing Congress's Commerce Clause power as plenary and limited only by other constitutional provisions).

[38] *See Quill*, 504 U.S. at 318 ("[O]ur decision is made easier by the fact that the underlying issue is not only one that Congress may be better qualified to resolve, but also one that Congress has the ultimate power to resolve. No matter how we evaluate the burdens that use taxes impose on interstate commerce, Congress remains free to disagree with our conclusions ... Accordingly, Congress is now free to decide whether, when, and to what extent the States may burden interstate mail-order concerns with a duty to collect use taxes.").

[39] Similar legislation has been introduced in prior Congresses. *See, e.g.*, S. 1736 and H.R. 3184 (108th Cong.)(allowing states to impose sales and use tax collection liability on large remote vendors once 10 states with at least 20% of the total population of all states with a sales tax became member states compliant with the Streamlined Sales and Use Tax Agreement and any necessary operational aspects of the Agreement were implemented).

[40] *See* STREAMLINED SALES TAX GOVERNING BOARD INC., *Frequently Asked Questions*, http://www.streamlinedsalestax.org/index.php?page=faqs [hereinafter *Streamlined Sales Tax FAQ*].

[41] For discussion of the agreement, see CRS Report R41853, *State Taxation of Internet Transactions*, by Steven Maguire.

[42] These 24 states are: Arkansas, Georgia, Indiana, Iowa, Kansas, Kentucky, Michigan, Minnesota, Nebraska, Nevada, New Jersey, North Carolina, North Dakota, Ohio, Oklahoma, Rhode Island, South Dakota, Tennessee, Utah, Vermont, Washington, West Virginia, Wisconsin and Wyoming. *See Streamlined Sales Tax FAQ, supra* note 40.

[43] According to the project's website, the 24 states that have enacted conforming legislation comprise 33% of the U.S. population. *See id.*

[44] *See* AMAZON ASSOCIATES, https://affiliate-program.amazon.com/gp/associates/join/landing/main.html.

[45] N.Y. TAX LAW §1101(b)(8)(i)(C)(I) (McKinney 2011).

[46] N.Y. TAX LAW §1101(b)(8)(vi) (McKinney 2011). For the presumption to apply, the cumulative gross receipts from sales by the seller to in-state customers as a result of all referrals must exceed $10,000 during the preceding four quarterly sales tax periods.

[47] New York State Dept. of Taxation and Finance, Office of Tax Policy Analysis, Taxpayer Guidance Division, *TSB-M08(3)S: New Presumption Applicable to Definition of Sales Tax Vendor* (May 8, 2008), available athttp://www.tax.ny.gov/pdf/memos/sales/m08_3s.pdf.

[48] *See id.*

[49] N.Y. TAX LAW §1101(b)(8)(vi) (McKinney 2011).

[50] Scripto, Inc. v. Carson, 362 U.S. 207, 211 (1960). *See also* Felt & Tarrant Co. v. Gallagher, 306 U.S. 62 (1939) (upholding state imposition of use tax collection liability on company with two agents in the state); General Trading Co. v. Tax Comm'n, 322 U.S. 335 (1944) (upholding state imposition of use tax collection liability on company with salespeople in the state).

[51] *See Scripto,* 362 U.S. at 211.

[52] *Id.*

[53] *Bellas Hess,* 386 U.S. at 757.

[54] *Cf. Quill,* 504 U.S. at 313 (imposing use tax collection liability was an impermissible burden on interstate commerce due to potential burden of such tax in light of the numerous taxing jurisdictions across the country).

[55] *See Amazon Laws: The Rise of "Click-thru Nexus" for Sales Tax Collection,* CBIZ (January 2011), available at http://www.cbiz.com/page.asp?pid=9111.

[56] Brief of Plaintiffs-Appellants, Amazon.com, LLC v. New York State Dep't of Taxation and Finance, 913 N.Y.S.2d 129 (N.Y. App. Div. 2010) (Nos. 1534, 1538), 2009 WL 7868633 at *24-25.

[57] Amazon.com LLC v. New York State Dep't of Taxation and Finance, 877 N.Y.S.2d 842, 846 (N.Y. Sup. Ct. 2009).

[58] Amazon.com, LLC v. New York State Dep't of Taxation and Finance, 913 N.Y.S.2d 129, 143, 144 (N.Y. App. Div. 2010) ("Inasmuch as there has been limited, if non-existent, discovery on issue we are unable to conclude as a matter of law that plaintiffs' in-state representatives are engaged in sufficiently meaningful activity [under the Commerce Clause] so as to implicate the State's taxing powers, and thus find that they should be given the opportunity to develop a record which establishes, actually, rather than theoretically, whether their in-state representatives are soliciting business or merely advertising on their behalf," and "we conclude that it would be premature to find that even as applied the due process challenges are unavailing, whether because they create an illegal and irrebuttable presumption, or because the language of the statute is so vague that plaintiffs cannot ascertain which transactions give rise to their obligations to collect the sales tax" and therefore "we remand for further discovery so that plaintiffs can make their record that all their in-state representatives do is advertise on New York-based Web sites.").

[59] *Id.* at 138.

[60] *See id.* at 139-40.

[61] COLO. REV. STAT. ANN. §39-21-112(3.5). "Retailer" is defined as "a person doing business in this state, known to the trade and public as such, and selling to the user or consumer, and not for resale." COLO. REV. STAT. ANN. §39-26-102(8). "Doing business in this state" is defined as "the selling, leasing, or delivering in this state, or any activity in this state in connection with the selling, leasing, or delivering in this state, of tangible personal property by a retail sale as defined in this section, for use, storage, distribution, or consumption within this state. This term includes, but shall not be limited to, the following acts or methods of transacting business:(a) The maintaining within this state, directly or indirectly or by a subsidiary, of an office, distributing house, salesroom or house, warehouse, or other place of business; (b)(I) The soliciting, either by direct representatives, indirect representatives, manufacturers' agents, or by distribution of catalogues or other advertising, or by use of any communication media, or by use of the newspaper, radio, or television advertising media, or by any other means whatsoever, of business from persons residing in this state and by reason thereof receiving orders from, or selling or leasing tangible personal property to, such persons residing in this state for use, consumption, distribution, and

storage for use or consumption in this state. (II) Commencing March 1, 2010, if a retailer that does not collect Colorado sales tax is part of a controlled group of corporations, and that controlled group has a component member that is a retailer with physical presence in this state, the retailer that does not collect Colorado sales tax is presumed to be doing business in this state ... This presumption may be rebutted by proof that during the calendar year in question, the component member that is a retailer with physical presence in this state did not engage in any constitutionally sufficient solicitation in this state on behalf of the retailer that does not collect Colorado sales tax." COLO. REV. STAT. ANN. §39-26-102(4).

[62] COLO. REV. STAT. ANN. §39-21-112(3.5)(c)(II), (d)(III)(A) and (B).

[63] *See* definitions *supra note* 59.

[64] Camps Newfound/Owatonna, Inc. v. Town of Harrison, 520 U.S. 564, 575 (1997) (internal citations omitted).

[65] New Energy Co. of Indiana v. Limbach, 486 U.S. 269, 278 (1988).

[66] Direct Mktg. Ass'n v. Huber, Civil Case No. 10-cv-01546-REB-CBS, 2012 U.S. Dist. LEXIS 44468 (D. Colo.March 30, 2012) (granting plaintiff's motion for summary judgment).

[67] *See id.* at *17-*20.

[68] *Id.* at 26.

[69] *See id.* at *26-*27.

In: Taxation of Internet Sales   ISBN: 978-1-62257-974-7
Editors: Keith Joyner and Carl Sawhill   © 2013 Nova Science Publishers, Inc.

Chapter 2

STATE TAXATION OF INTERNET TRANSACTIONS*

Steven Maguire

SUMMARY

The United States Bureau of the Census estimated that $3.4 trillion worth of retail and wholesale transactions were conducted over the Internet in 2009. That amount was 16.8% of all U.S. shipments and sales in that year. Other estimates projected the 2011 so-called e-commerce volume at approximately $3.9 trillion. The volume of e-commerce is expected to increase and state and local governments are concerned because collection of sales taxes on these transactions is difficult to enforce.

Under current law, states cannot reach beyond their borders and compel out-of-state Internet vendors (those without nexus in the buyer's state) to collect the use tax owed by state residents and businesses. The Supreme Court ruled in 1967 that requiring remote vendors to collect the use tax would pose an undue burden on interstate commerce. Estimates put this lost tax revenue at approximately $11.4 billion in 2012.

Congress is involved because interstate commerce typically falls under the Commerce Clause of the Constitution. Opponents of remote vendor sales and use tax collection cite the complexity of the myriad state and local sales tax

* This is an edited, reformatted and augmented version of the Congressional Research Service Publication, CRS Report for Congress R41853, dated December 8, 2011.

systems and the difficulty vendors would have in collecting and remitting use taxes. Proponents would like Congress to change the law and allow states to require out-of-state vendors without nexus to collect state use taxes. These proponents acknowledge that simplification and harmonization of state tax systems are likely prerequisites for Congress to consider approval of increased collection authority for states.

A number of states have been working together to harmonize sales tax collection and have created the Streamlined Sales and Use Tax Agreement (SSUTA). The SSUTA member states hope that Congress can be persuaded to allow them to require out-of-state vendors to collect taxes from customers in SSUTA member states.

In the 112th Congress, S. 1452 and H.R. 2701 (Senator Durbin and Representative Conyers) would grant SSUTA member states the authority to compel out-of-state vendors in other member states to collect sales and use taxes. In addition, H.R. 3179 (Representative Womack) would also grant states the authority to compel out-of-state vendors to collect use taxes provided selected simplification efforts are implemented. S. 1832 (Senator Enzi and others including Senator Durbin) would grant SSUTA member states and non-member states that meet less rigorous simplifications standards the authority to compel out-of-state vendors to collect sales and use taxes.

A related issue is the "Internet Tax Moratorium." The relatively narrow moratorium prohibits (1) new taxes on Internet access services and (2) multiple or discriminatory taxes on Internet commerce. Congress has extended the "Internet Tax Moratorium" twice. The most recent extension expires November 1, 2014. The moratorium is distinct from the remote use tax collection issue, but has been linked in past debates. An analysis of the Internet tax moratorium is beyond the scope of this report.

INTRODUCTION

State governments rely on general sales and use taxes for just under one-third (32.0%) of their total tax revenue—approximately $223 billion in FY2009. Local governments derive 11.2% of their tax revenue—approximately $62 billion in FY2009—from general sales and use taxes. Both state and local sales taxes are usually collected by vendors at the point of transaction and levied as a percentage of a product's retail price. Alternatively, use taxes, levied at the same rate, are often not collected by the vendor if the vendor does not have nexus (loosely defined as a physical presence) in the consumer's state. Consumers are required to remit use taxes to their taxing jurisdiction for the use of the product purchased. Compliance with this requirement, however, is quite low.

State and local governments are concerned that the expansion of e-commerce, which is estimated to reach approximately $3.9 trillion in 2011, is gradually eroding their tax base.[1] This concern arises in part because the U.S. Supreme Court ruled out-of-state vendors are not required to collect sales taxes for states in which they (the vendors) do not have nexus. In hopes of stemming the potential loss of tax revenue, several states are participating in an initiative to simplify and coordinate their tax codes—called the Streamlined Sales and Use Tax Agreement (SSUTA). The member states hope that Congress could be persuaded to allow them to require out-of-state vendors to collect taxes from resident customers.

Congress has a role in this issue because interstate commerce, in most cases, falls under the Commerce Clause of the Constitution. Congress will likely be asked to choose between taking either an active or passive role in the debate. In the 112th Congress, S. 1452 and H.R. 2701 (Senator Durbin and Representative Conyers) would grant SSUTA member states the authority to compel out-of-state vendors in other member states to collect sales and use taxes. On the House side, H.R. 3179 (Representative Womack) would also grant states the authority to compel out-of-state vendors to collect use taxes provided selected simplification efforts are implemented. S. 1832 (Senator Enzi and others including Senator Durbin) would grant SSUTA member states and non-member states that meet less rigorous simplifications standards the authority to compel out-of-state vendors to collect sales and use taxes.

In the 111th Congress, H.R. 5660 (former Representative Delahunt) would have granted SSUTA member states the authority to compel out-of-state vendors to collect sales and use taxes. A more passive approach by Congress could involve states implementing the SSUTA without congressional approval. State enforcement of remote collection would likely face legal challenges, and the outcome of these legal challenges is uncertain. This report intends to clarify significant issues in the remote sales tax collection debate, beginning with a description of state and local sales and use taxes.

The impact of congressional action (or inaction) on the remote collection issue will vary significantly by state. For this reason, the report includes a state-by-state analysis of the sales tax.

STATE AND LOCAL SALES AND USE TAXES

In 1932, Mississippi was the first state to impose a general state sales tax. During the remainder of the 1930s, an era characterized by declining revenue from corporate and individual income taxes, 23 other states followed suit and implemented a general sales tax. At the time, the sales tax was relatively easy to administer and raised a significant amount of revenue despite a relatively low rate. Given the relative success of the sales tax in raising revenue, 45 states and the District of Columbia added the sales tax to their tax infrastructure by the late 1960s. The last of the 45 states to enact a general sales and use tax was Vermont in 1969.

Components of the Sales and Use Tax

The revenue generated by a sales and use tax, assuming a given level of compliance, depends on the base of the tax and the tax rate. States often have similar consumption items included in their tax base, but they are far from uniform. Tax rates can also vary considerably, depending on the state's reliance on other revenue sources. The SSUTA is intended to provide uniform definitions across states for items included in the base and the applicable tax rates. Following is an analysis of the variation of these components across the states.

Tax Base

The sales tax is perhaps better identified as a transaction tax on the transfer of tangible personal property, as expenditures on most services are typically excluded from the state sales tax base. In addition, in most states (34) and the District of Columbia, groceries are also exempt from state and local sales taxes or taxed at a lower rate.[2]

Table 1 presents the most recently available data on state and local tax revenue and an estimate of each state's sales tax base. The sales tax revenue includes collections from individuals as well as businesses. The estimate of the sales tax base as a share of income is a rough approximation of the state sales tax base.[3] A higher percentage likely indicates (1) a greater number of items and services subject to the sales and (2) greater compliance. In the case of Hawaii, where over 100% of personal income is includable in the tax base, the percentage likely measures some degree of pyramiding of the sales tax. Pyramiding occurs when a business pays sales tax on a good then collects more sales tax when the good is sold. Pyramiding is common in many other states, but is difficult to quantify. In total, roughly half of personal income is spent on items subject to the sales taxes.

Table 1. State and Local Sales Taxes as Percentage of Total Personal Income, 2009
(amounts in thousands of dollars; tax data are FY2009)

State	Total State and Local Sales Taxes FY2009	State Sales Taxes FY2009	Local Sales Taxes FY2009	State Personal Income 2009	Sales Tax Base as Share of Income[a]
United States	291,045,219	228,728,864	62,316,355	11,916,808,000	49.5%
Alabama	3,870,370	2,069,535	1,800,835	155,399,306	43.2%
Alaska	201,285	-	201,285	30,215,480	—
Arizona	7,404,971	4,878,883	2,526,088	215,397,567	47.3%
Arkansas	3,672,902	2,765,996	906,906	92,609,959	63.2%
California	37,319,859	28,972,302	8,347,557	1,528,457,253	39.4%
Colorado	5,063,670	2,123,671	2,939,999	205,437,450	44.6%
Connecticut	3,290,050	3,290,050	-	190,817,959	40.9%
Delaware	-	-	-	34,444,313	—
Florida	849,316	(X)	849,316	40,138,076	55.7%
Georgia	20,595,437	19,228,000	1,367,437	697,362,360	51.7%
Hawaii	8,981,969	5,306,491	3,675,478	327,892,184	101.3%
Idaho	2,461,618	2,461,618	-	54,785,668	50.4%
Illinois	1,206,137	1,206,137	-	48,236,239	31.8%
Indiana	10,788,266	9,355,421	1,432,845	525,411,146	44.2%
Iowa	6,205,638	6,205,638	-	215,502,883	44.5%
Kansas	2,808,415	2,201,396	607,019	112,442,136	50.2%
Kentucky	2,954,960	2,227,183	727,777	108,340,102	46.1%
Louisiana	2,857,665	2,857,665	-	137,958,755	63.6%
Maine	6,650,163	2,963,758	3,686,405	162,402,480	48.4%
Maryland	1,012,357	1,012,357	-	47,941,898	34.7%
Massachusetts	3,851,341	3,851,341	-	273,193,372	29.3%
Michigan	3,880,087	3,880,087	-	324,680,171	50.1%
Minnesota	8,998,942	8,998,942	-	331,846,696	43.5%
Mississippi	4,488,981	4,375,200	113,781	217,704,595	55.6%
Missouri	3,026,497	3,026,497	-	88,779,546	46.8%
Montana	4,801,433	3,030,477	1,770,956	216,049,019	—
Nebraska	-	-	-	33,168,003	44.4%
Nevada	1,795,820	1,504,174	291,646	70,072,173	57.0%

Table 1. (Continued)

State	Total State and Local Sales Taxes FY2009	State Sales Taxes FY2009	Local Sales Taxes FY2009	State Personal Income 2009	Sales Tax Base as Share of Income[a]
New Hampshire[b]	2,995,944	2,684,029	311,915	98,041,013	—
New Jersey	-	-	-	55,858,973	28.8%
New Mexico	8,188,990	8,188,990	-	433,996,947	89.3%
New York	2,708,363	1,881,651	826,712	65,980,486	34.4%
North Carolina	22,534,922	11,073,898	11,461,024	901,615,996	44.9%
North Dakota	7,366,717	4,963,434	2,403,283	322,307,163	52.9%
Ohio	705,296	607,171	98,125	26,361,749	39.1%
Oklahoma	8,986,115	7,328,388	1,657,727	405,184,176	67.4%
Oregon	3,755,229	2,162,693	1,592,536	126,412,117	—
Pennsylvania	-	-	-	135,474,469	32.6%
Rhode Island	8,804,969	8,496,182	308,787	499,330,513	28.2%
South Carolina	814,511	814,511	-	42,889,454	53.1%
South Dakota	3,129,633	2,910,183	219,450	145,249,286	68.8%
Tennessee[b]	1,034,862	756,598	278,264	30,861,923	52.3%
Texas	8,299,190	6,356,962	1,942,228	213,155,957	48.5%
Utah	26,545,052	21,053,923	5,491,129	904,212,180	60.7%
Vermont	2,348,870	1,744,035	604,835	86,838,578	40.3%
Virginia	329,031	321,162	7,869	24,273,382	42.3%
Washington	4,405,279	3,372,974	1,032,305	342,297,555	48.0%
West Virginia	12,329,189	10,035,359	2,293,830	278,665,083	48.5%
Wisconsin	1,110,017	1,110,017	-	57,419,415	46.3%
Wyoming	4,396,601	4,084,147	312,454	209,347,374	75.1%

Source: U.S. Bureau of Census, State and Local Government Finances by Level of Government and by State: 2008-09, available at http://www.census.gov/govs/ estimate/.

Notes: States in italics are states without a broad-based income tax.

a. Mikesell, John, "Retail Sales Taxes, 1995-98: An Era Ends," *State Tax Notes*, February 21, 2000, p. 594. Data are for the 1998 tax year, the latest year for which estimates of sales tax base were made.

b. New Hampshire and Tennessee levy a tax on income from dividends and interest.

Tax Rate

The second component of a sales tax is the tax rate applied to the base. In 34 states, local governments piggy-back a local sales tax (which often varies among localities within the state) on the state sales tax; 11 states and the District of Columbia levy a single rate (see **Table 2**), with no local taxes. Some states in the group of 34 may collect a uniform local tax along with the state tax and send the local revenue share back to the localities. This structure would look like a single rate to the consumer because vendors typically do not differentiate between the state and local share. For example, vendors in Virginia levy a 5.0% sales tax on purchases and remit the entire amount to the state. The state then returns what would have been raised by a 1.0% tax back to the local jurisdiction where the tax was collected. The state of Virginia keeps the remaining 4.0%.

As of January 1, 2011, California had the highest state sales tax rate of 7.25%. Indiana, Mississippi, New Jersey, Rhode Island, and Tennessee had state sales tax rate of 7.0%. The state rate is only part of the total rate; as noted earlier, most states also levy a local sales tax. As of January 1, 2011, Arizona had the highest potential combined state and local rate of 12.1%, with Alabama second at 12.0%.

Residents in high sales tax rate jurisdictions could benefit more from Internet purchases (and tax evasion) relative to those in low tax rate states. Recognizing this potential revenue loss, many high-rate states have stepped up efforts to inform consumers of their responsibility to pay use taxes on Internet and mail-order catalog purchases. As suggested earlier, states with high rates— and whose residents have a greater incentive to evade taxes—are exposed to greater potential revenue losses from the growth of Internet commerce. Because of the greater potential losses, these states are more likely to support reforms that help maintain their sales and use tax revenue base.

The tax base and tax rate determine how much revenue is generated by the sales tax for each jurisdiction. The share lost to non-compliance arising from e-commerce, however, varies considerably by state. Part of the variance can be attributed to the two components of the overall compliance: sales tax collected by vendors and use tax remitted by purchasers. Researchers on e-commerce estimated a relatively high vendor compliance though considerably lower purchaser compliance.[4]

Table 2 also lists each state's current status with the SSUTA. The "member" states (20) have all enacted laws that fully comply with the SSUTA. A second group of states (4) are considered "associate" states and not full members because relatively small technical changes are needed in state tax laws to be in full compliance with SSUTA. A third group of states (19) are participating in the streamlining effort but have not made the necessary uniformity changes in state sales tax law to be considered for member or associate status.

Table 2. SSUTA Status and State and Local Sales Tax Rates

State	SSUTA Status[a]	State Tax Rate[b]	Top Local Rate[b]	Maximum Combined	Rank
United States Average	—	5.047%	2.547%	7.594%	—
Alabama	Advisory	4.000%	8.000%	12.000%	2
Alaska	No Sales Tax	—	7.500%	7.500%	28
Arizona	Advisory	6.600%	5.500%	12.100%	1
Arkansas	Member	6.000%	5.500%	11.500%	3
California	Advisory	8.250%	3.000%	11.250%	5
Colorado	Non-Participant	2.900%	7.000%	9.900%	12
Connecticut	Advisory	6.000%	—	6.000%	38
Delaware	No Sales Tax	—	—	—	47
Florida	Advisory	6.000%	1.500%	7.500%	28
Georgia	Associate	4.000%	4.000%	8.000%	21
Hawaii	Advisory	4.000%	0.500%	4.500%	46
Idaho	Not Advisory	6.000%	3.000%	9.000%	15
Illinois	Advisory	6.250%	4.250%	10.500%	10
Indiana	Member	7.000%	—	7.000%	32
Iowa	Member	6.000%	2.000%	8.000%	21
Kansas	Member	6.300%	5.000%	11.300%	4
Kentucky	Member	6.000%	—	6.000%	38
Louisiana	Advisory	4.000%	6.750%	10.750%	8
Maine	Advisory	5.000%	—	5.000%	44
Maryland	Advisory	6.000%	—	6.000%	38
Massachusetts	Advisory	6.250%	—	6.250%	37
Michigan	Member	6.000%	—	6.000%	38
Minnesota	Member	6.875%	1.000%	7.875%	25
Mississippi	Advisory	7.000%	0.250%	7.250%	31
Missouri	Advisory	4.225%	6.625%	10.850%	6
Montana	No Sales Tax	—	—	—	47
Nebraska	Member	5.500%	2.000%	7.500%	28
Nevada	Member	6.850%	1.250%	8.100%	20
New Hampshire	No Sales Tax	—	—	—	47
New Jersey	Member	7.000%	—	7.000%	32
New Mexico	Advisory	5.125%	5.625%	10.750%	9
New York	Advisory	4.000%	5.000%	9.000%	15
North Carolina	Member	5.750%	3.000%	8.750%	18
North Dakota	Member	5.000%	2.500%	7.500%	27
Ohio	Associate	5.500%	2.250%	7.750%	26

State	SSUTA Status[a]	State Tax Rate[b]	Top Local Rate[b]	Maximum Combined	Rank
Oklahoma	Member	4.500%	6.350%	10.850%	7
Oregon	No Sales Tax	—	—	—	47
Pennsylvania	Not Advisory	6.000%	2.000%	8.000%	21
Rhode Island	Member	7.000%	0.000%	7.000%	32
South Carolina	Advisory	6.000%	3.000%	9.000%	15
South Dakota	Member	4.000%	2.000%	6.000%	38
Tennessee	Associate	7.000%	2.750%	9.750%	13
Texas	Advisory	6.250%	2.000%	8.250%	19
Utah	Associate	4.700%	5.250%	9.950%	11
Vermont	Member	6.000%	1.000%	7.000%	35
Virginia	Advisory	4.000%	1.000%	5.000%	44
Washington	Member	6.500%	3.000%	9.500%	14
West Virginia	Member	6.000%	—	6.000%	38
Wisconsin	Member	5.000%	1.500%	6.500%	36
Wyoming	Member	4.000%	4.000%	8.000%	21

Source: State and local sales tax rate data are from the Sales Tax Institute at http://www.salestaxinstitute.com/resources/rates. The highest combined rate and accompanying rank is a CRS calculation.

Notes: "Member" means full participant in SSUTA; "Associate" generally means technical changes need in state tax laws for state full conformity; "Advisory" means not conforming to SSTUA; "Not Advisory" means part of the project, but not advising decisions; and "Non-participating" means state is not working with other states toward conformity.

a. Status is as of January 1, 2011.

b. State and local sales tax rate data are as of May 1, 2011.

State Reliance on Sales Taxes

In addition to a sales tax, most states levy income taxes and almost every local jurisdiction (and some states) also levies a property tax. **Table 3** presents the relative reliance of each state and local government combined on the three principal revenue sources: sales taxes, income taxes, and property taxes. Reliance is measured as a percentage of total taxes collected. Other taxes include selective sales taxes such as motor fuels taxes, alcoholic beverages taxes, tobacco product taxes, and corporate income taxes.

The U.S. average reliance is greatest for the property tax at 33.4%, and the sales tax and individual income tax accounted for 22.9% and 21.3%, respectively, of tax revenue in FY2009. The top three states in sales tax reliance were Tennessee, Washington, and South Dakota. These three states do not levy a broad based income tax, thus increasing their reliance on sales taxes.[5]

Table 3. State and Local Government Sales Tax Reliance (FY2009)

State	Total Taxes	Sales Tax Reliance Rank	General Sales Tax	Income Tax	Property Tax	Other Taxes
United States	1,271,355,992		22.9%	21.3%	33.4%	22.5%
Alabama	13,349,221	15	29.0%	20.9%	17.9%	32.2%
Alaska	6,358,792	47	3.2%	-	18.8%	78.0%
Arizona	20,645,411	8	35.9%	12.5%	34.2%	17.5%
Arkansas	9,425,428	4	39.0%	23.8%	16.8%	20.5%
California	169,593,984	28	22.0%	26.2%	31.8%	20.1%
Colorado	18,748,462	17	27.0%	23.5%	33.6%	15.9%
Connecticut	21,092,339	42	15.6%	26.6%	41.7%	16.1%
Delaware	3,594,071	48	0.0%	26.9%	17.6%	55.5%
District of Columbia	5,013,075	39	16.9%	22.5%	35.7%	24.9%
Florida	68,605,386	13	30.0%	0.0%	43.1%	26.9%
Georgia	31,509,607	16	28.5%	24.8%	33.1%	13.6%
Hawaii	6,389,452	6	38.5%	21.0%	20.6%	19.9%
Idaho	4,520,747	19	26.7%	26.0%	27.8%	19.5%
Illinois	56,770,773	32	19.0%	16.2%	40.1%	24.7%
Indiana	23,876,218	20	26.0%	23.9%	30.3%	19.8%
Iowa	11,892,338	26	23.6%	23.5%	33.2%	19.7%
Kansas	11,471,073	21	25.8%	23.8%	33.3%	17.1%
Kentucky	13,859,499	30	20.6%	31.3%	20.6%	27.5%
Louisiana	17,477,717	7	38.0%	16.8%	17.9%	27.2%
Maine	5,651,435	35	17.9%	24.3%	38.6%	19.2%
Maryland	26,977,340	43	14.3%	39.9%	25.5%	20.4%
Massachusetts	32,270,716	45	12.0%	32.8%	37.7%	17.4%
Michigan	35,913,855	22	25.1%	17.5%	40.1%	17.3%
Minnesota	24,023,936	33	18.7%	28.9%	29.5%	22.9%
Mississippi	9,000,910	9	33.6%	16.5%	26.0%	23.8%
Missouri	19,219,438	23	25.0%	26.4%	28.7%	19.9%
Montana	3,487,845	48	0.0%	23.7%	36.6%	39.7%
Nebraska	7,352,002	24	24.4%	21.8%	35.3%	18.5%
Nevada	10,132,795	14	29.6%	0.0%	34.7%	35.7%
New Hampshire	4,987,644	48	0.0%	2.0%	64.4%	33.6%

State	Total Taxes	Sales Tax Reliance Rank	General Sales Tax	Income Tax	Property Tax	Other Taxes
New Jersey	50,919,922	41	16.1%	20.9%	45.7%	17.3%
New Mexico	6,998,589	5	38.7%	13.7%	17.5%	30.1%
New York	135,494,886	40	16.6%	32.8%	30.4%	20.2%
North Carolina	31,657,814	27	23.3%	30.2%	25.7%	20.8%
North Dakota	3,314,044	29	21.3%	11.2%	23.2%	44.3%
Ohio	43,949,000	31	20.4%	28.7%	29.8%	21.1%
Oklahoma	12,236,802	11	30.7%	20.8%	18.0%	30.5%
Oregon	12,473,614	48	0.0%	41.4%	35.6%	23.0%
Pennsylvania	51,918,267	38	17.0%	25.8%	29.9%	27.3%
Rhode Island	4,765,746	37	17.1%	20.2%	44.6%	18.1%
South Carolina	13,087,110	25	23.9%	21.5%	33.8%	20.8%
South Dakota	2,554,807	3	40.5%	0.0%	34.9%	24.6%
Tennessee	17,886,843	1	46.4%	1.2%	26.3%	26.1%
Texas	86,232,402	10	30.8%	0.0%	42.0%	27.2%
Utah	8,728,976	18	26.9%	26.6%	26.6%	19.9%
Vermont	2,904,321	46	11.3%	18.3%	44.2%	26.1%
Virginia	31,464,327	44	14.0%	29.2%	35.8%	20.9%
Washington	26,980,749	2	45.7%	0.0%	30.0%	24.3%
West Virginia	6,406,512	36	17.3%	24.3%	20.4%	38.0%
Wisconsin	24,124,990	34	18.2%	24.8%	38.3%	18.8%
Wyoming	4,044,764	12	30.1%	0.0%	31.2%	38.6%

Source: CRS calculations based on U.S. Bureau of Census, State and Local Government Finances by
   Level of Government and by State: 2007-08, available at http://www.census.gov/govs/estimate/.
Note: New Hampshire and Tennessee levy a tax on income from dividends and interest.

DESCRIPTION OF THE SSUTA

The entity that drafted the original Streamline Sales and Use Tax Agreement (SSUTA), the Streamlined Sales and Use Tax Project (SSTP), was created in 2000 by 43 states and the District of Columbia. These states and the District of Columbia wanted to simplify and better synchronize individual state sales and use tax laws. Its stated goal was to create a simplified sales tax system so all types of vendors—from traditional retailers to those conducting trade over the Internet— could easily collect and remit sales taxes. The member states believe that a simplified, relatively uniform tax code across states would make it easier for remote vendors to collect sales taxes on goods sold to out-of-state customers. The SSTP was dissolved once the SSUTA became effective on October 1, 2005. The latest amendments to the SSUTA were approved May 19, 2011.[6]

The SSUTA agreement explicitly identifies 10 points of focus.[7] Uniformity and simplification are the primary themes with state level administration of the sales and use tax a critical element in achieving the "streamlining" goal. The 10 points of focus can be condensed into four general requirements for simplification: (1) state level administration, (2) uniform tax base, (3) simplified tax rates, and (4) uniform sales sourcing rules. Each is discussed in more detail in the following sections.

State Level Administration

Administration of the sales tax for multistate businesses is complicated because state sales tax laws are not uniform.[8] Currently, multistate businesses file sales tax returns for each jurisdiction in which they are required to remit sales taxes. These state sales and use tax compliance rules are far from uniform, which increases compliance costs and the accompanying economic inefficiencies.

Under SSUTA, sales taxes would be remitted to a single state agency and businesses will no longer file tax returns with each state (and sometimes local jurisdiction) where they conduct business. States would bear some of the administrative cost of the technology employed to implement the new system.

States also would incur some additional administrative costs through vendor collection incentives. State and local governments currently compensate vendors for collection under a variety of rules and rates. Total vendor compensation would be somewhat standardized under SSUTA with three uniform brackets with rates set by each member state. SSUTA would require that rates decline as a business's tax collection volume increases. Total compensation for vendors in member states that require tax reporting by local jurisdiction is at least 0.75% of state and local sales and use tax collections. Total compensation for vendors in member states that *do not require* tax reporting by local jurisdiction is a minimum of 0.5% of sales and use tax collections.

As of this writing, 20 states were in full compliance with the terms of the SSUTA and are identified as "members." Another four states are "associate members." Only the member states will have taxes collected by remote vendors. **Table 2** lists the status of SSUTA adoption in each state.

Uniform Tax Base

As noted earlier, each state has established rules for what to include in the sales tax base, and definitions of these items are not uniform across states. The SSUTA includes a section requiring that within each state, all jurisdictions use the same tax base.[9] Thus, if the state excludes groceries from the sales tax, all local governments within the state must also exclude groceries. This seemingly straightforward requirement can become complicated. For example, as noted above, groceries are exempt from taxation in most states, whereas candy is taxable in several states. A common definition of candy (or food) must be agreed upon to implement a streamlined sales tax regime. Under SSUTA,

> "Candy" means a preparation of sugar, honey, or other natural or artificial sweeteners in combination with chocolate, fruits, nuts or other ingredients or flavorings in the form of bars, drops, or pieces. "Candy" shall not include any preparation containing flour and shall require no refrigeration.

Each state would retain the choice over whether the item is taxable (in the base) and the rate that applies to the product.

Simplified Tax Rates

In many states, local jurisdictions tax goods at different rates. This complication is mostly remedied under the SSUTA, as each state would be permitted only one state tax rate (with an exception for a second state rate on food and drugs). Each state can add one additional local jurisdiction rate, based on ZIP code. The member state must maintain a catalogue of rates for all ZIP codes. For ZIP codes with multiple rates, an average rate for that ZIP code would apply.

Standard Rate Sourcing Rules for Cross-Jurisdictional Sales

Sourcing rules for sales within a member state between local jurisdictions, the vendor would collect the sales tax at the rate applicable for the vendor location. This is identified as "origin" sourcing. For sales into a member state from an out-of-state vendor, the vendor levies a tax at the agreed upon statewide rate applicable in the destination state. This is identified as "destination" sourcing and is the general rule under the SSUTA.

There is some debate about the "sourcing" aspect of the SSUTA. The single statewide rate, which is set by each member state, would be a combined state and local rate. If the combined statewide rate is the state rate plus an average of local rates, it is possible that some consumers will pay a higher combined tax rate than is required. It has been proposed that the member states would be required to include a provision in the implementing legislation that would allow consumers that "overpay" to receive a credit for overpayments.

SSUTA Stakeholders

The SSUTA enjoys the support of the National Governors Association (NGA). The NGA has endorsed the SSUTA with hopes that the agreement will address the Supreme Court's concerns about the burden on interstate commerce of collecting remote taxes. The association believes that requiring remote vendors to collect sales and use taxes under a new, simplified system will survive legal challenges. The official statement of the NGA position on the efforts to streamline state and local taxes begins with the following:

> The National Governors Association supports state efforts to pursue, through negotiations, the courts, and federal legislation, provisions that would require remote, out-of-state vendors to collect sales and use taxes from their customers. Such action is necessary to restore fairness between local retail store purchases and remote sellers and to provide a means for the states to collect taxes that are owed under existing law. The rapid growth of the Internet and electronic commerce underscores the importance of maintaining equitable treatment among all sellers.[10]

The NGA support is shared by other state and local government organizations, including the National Conference of State Legislatures (NCSL), the Federation of Tax Administrators (FTA), and the Multistate Tax Commission (MTC).

Support also comes from large retailers who must collect sales taxes and believe the current system provides an unfair advantage to Internet retailers who do not collect such taxes. Many large brick-and-mortar companies with a strong Internet presence generally comply with guidelines like those under

SSUTA and generally collect taxes on remote sales. Several retailers, however, are taking the middle ground in this debate. They understand the states' desire to more efficiently collect sales tax revenue in a fair manner, but they ask for greater simplification and increased vendor compensation from the states for collecting state sales taxes.

Opponents of SSUTA legislation include state and local governments who feel the administrative obstacles to streamlined sales taxes are too costly to overcome and may actually exceed the potential revenue gain. These governments suggest that increased compliance with use tax laws may better be achieved through elevated consumer awareness and more enforcement activities. In addition, some business groups maintain that the collection requirement, even with streamlining, would still be too burdensome.

Also opposing SSUTA legislation are several anti-tax groups who see the SSUTA as a new tax burden rather than a simplification of the current tax system. Anti-tax groups also argue that states compete to attract businesses and customers through lower tax rates and that this competition is good for consumers.

CONGRESSIONAL AND STATE LEGISLATIVE ACTIVITY

Remote seller collection legislation at the federal level includes bills requiring SSUTA adoption and bills that are not conditioned on SSUTA approval. State efforts have taken two tracks: adopting SSUTA type legislation and/or implementing so-called Amazon laws. Following is a brief discussion of this activity.

SSUTA Legislation

In the 112th Congress, S. 1452 and H.R. 2701 would grant SSUTA member states the authority to compel out-of-state vendors in member states to collect sales and use taxes.[11] The legislation would have responded to the Supreme Court's recommendation in *Quill Corporation v. North Dakota* that Congress act, under the Commerce Clause, to clarify state sales tax collection rules. More specifically, the legislation would have allowed states that have fully adopted the SSUTA to collect sales taxes from sufficiently large businesses, even if those businesses do not have a nexus in the state. A "sufficiently large business" is left to the governing board of the SSUTA to define.

Under S. 1452, Congress would grant authority to states to compel out-of-state vendors to collect sales taxes, on the condition that 10 states comprising at least 20% of the total population of all states imposing a sales tax have implemented the SSUTA. The legislation also includes additional requirements for administering the new sales tax system after the SSUTA adoption threshold has been achieved. These requirements included, but were not limited to,

- a centralized, one-stop multi-state registration system;
- uniform definitions of products and product-based exemptions;
- single tax rate per taxing jurisdiction with a single additional rate for food and drugs;
- single, state-level administration of sales and use taxes;
- uniform rules for sourcing (i.e., the tax rate imposed is based on the origin or destination of the product);
- uniform procedures for certification of tax information service providers;
- uniform rules for filing returns and performing audits; and
- reasonable compensation for sellers collecting and remitting taxes.

The SSUTA generally includes these provisions, though some modifications to the SSUTA or the legislation may be necessary for enactment.

Under the SSUTA, member states request that remote sellers voluntarily collect sales taxes on items purchased by customers outside their home state. Vendors in participating states who voluntarily collect the sales tax would be offered amnesty for previously uncollected taxes. Participating states have agreed to share the administrative burden of collecting taxes to ease tax collection for sellers. The states' obligations under the SSUTA include the following requirements.

Business-to-business transactions are often exempt from the retail sales tax, particularly in cases where the purchaser is using the good as an input to production. These transactions are exempt because including the transactions could lead to the "pyramiding" of the sales tax. For example, if a coffee shop were to pay a retail sales tax on the purchase of coffee, and then impose a retail sales tax on coffee brewed for the final consumer, the total sales tax paid for the cup of coffee would likely exceed the statutory rate. Products that a business purchases for resale are typically not assessed a retail sales tax for a similar reason. If a coffee shop buys beans only for resale, levying a sales tax on the wholesale purchase of the beans and then on the retail sale would more than double the statutory rate. The tax treatment of business purchases is not uniform across states. According to some estimates, approximately 18% of business purchases are taxable depending on the state.

Many individuals and organizations are also exempt from state sales taxes. Entities wishing to claim the sales tax exemption are often issued a certificate indicating their tax-free status and are required to present this certification at the point of transaction. Non-profit organizations, such as those whose mission is religious, charitable, educational, or promoting public health, often hold sales tax-exempt status.

The SSUTA would establish a system in which states would use common definitions for goods and services. Once a uniform definition is established, states would then indicate whether the good or service is taxable. In addition, states would identify which entities would be exempt from paying sales taxes (e.g., non-profit or religious organizations).

Other Remote Seller Sales Tax Collection Legislation

In the 112th Congress, H.R. 3179, the Market Place Equity Act of 2011, introduced by Representative Womack and S. 1832 (Senator Enzi) would attempt to achieve the same policy objective without a formal multistate compact like SSUTA. Instead, H.R. 3179 would authorize states to compel out-of-state vendors to collect sales and use taxes if the following requirements were satisfied:

- the state creates a remote seller sales and use tax return and requires filing no more frequently than in-state vendors;
- the state maintains a uniform tax base across the state;
- the state uses one of three structures for remote sales tax collection: (1) a single state and local "blended" rate, (2) a single maximum state rate exclusive of any additional local rates, or (3) the destination rate which would be the actual rate of the customer's jurisdiction.

In addition, a final condition requires that the rates determined in (1) and (2) above cannot exceed the average rate applicable to in-state vendors. For purposes of (3), the state must provide vendors access to a tax rate database for all jurisdictions. Remote vendors with total United States remote sales under $1 million or remote vendors with less than $100,000 in a given state, are exempt from collection responsibility.

Like H.R. 3179, S. 1832 would allow remote collection authority for non-SSUTA states if minimum simplification requirements are achieved. Following is a brief summary of key simplification requirements for Congress to grant collection authority under S. 1832:

- provide a single state-level agency to administer and audit sales tax returns;
- provide a single sales and use tax return for vendors;
- provide a uniform sales tax base for all jurisdictions within the state;
- set tax rates at the combined state and local sales tax rate where the goods or taxable services are delivered (the destination rate);
- provide remote vendors with "adequate" software for determining the appropriate destination rate.

S. 1832 would establish a small seller exception for vendors with less than $500,000 in U.S. Internet sales. The legislation also includes a provision to limit the collections authority to just sales tax and not the imposition or application of other taxes such as franchise, income, and occupation taxes.

Amazon Laws

Some states have begun to enact what are called "Amazon Laws." The "Amazon" modifier refers to the large Internet retailer that is located in Washington State. Amazon collects sales taxes only in the states where they claim their presence legally requires collection. In addition to Washington State, Amazon reportedly collects sales taxes in these additional states: Kansas, Kentucky, New York, and North Dakota.[12] At issue are affiliate agreements between Amazon and retailers that provide an Internet portal to Amazon. Typically, the affiliates are compensated for transactions that result from the so-called "click through" to Amazon.

New York State, the first to enact a so-called Amazon Law in 2008, claimed that the affiliate relationship constituted physical presence for Amazon.[13] Along with the physical presence established by the affiliate relationship came responsibility for collecting sales taxes on products sold to New York residents by Amazon. Several legal challenges to these so-called

Amazon laws have been presented; a thorough legal analysis of these challenges extends beyond the scope of this report. Some proponents of the SSUTA see the growth of Amazon Laws as possibly complicating simplification efforts. Recently, Amazon has indicated support for congressionally approved collection authority as provided for in the legislation described in this report, with some modifications.[14]

ECONOMIC ISSUES

During the debate about so-called "streamlining" legislation, there are several economic issues Congress may consider: (1) How will the SSUTA influence the economic efficiency and equity of state tax systems? (2) What will be the impact of changes in the treatment of Internet transactions on states that are more reliant on the sales tax? (3) What will the potential revenue loss be, absent changes in the treatment of Internet transactions? A summary of these issues follows.

Efficiency

A commonly held view among economists is that a "good" tax (or more precisely, an efficient tax) minimizes distortions in consumer behavior. Broadly speaking, economists maintain that individuals should make the same choices before and after a tax is imposed. The greater the distortions in behavior caused by a tax, the greater the economic welfare loss. A sales tax levied on all consumer expenditures equally would satisfy this definition of efficiency. As noted earlier, however, under the current state sales tax system, all consumption expenditures are not treated equally. The growth of tax-free Internet transactions, both business-to-business and business-to-consumer, will likely amplify the efficiency losses from altered consumer behavior.

An alternative theory concerning economic efficiency in sales taxation is referred to as "optimal commodity taxation." Under an optimal commodity tax, the tax rate is based on (or determined by) what is termed the price elasticity of demand for the product (sometimes called the "Ramsey Rule"). Products that are price inelastic, meaning quantity demanded is unresponsive to changes in price, should be levied a higher rate of tax. In contrast, products that are price elastic should have a lower rate of tax. If products purchased over the Internet are relatively more price elastic, then the lower tax rate created by effectively tax-free Internet transactions may improve economic efficiency as behavioral changes are reduced. However, the price elasticity of products available over the Internet is difficult to measure and the efficiency gain, if any, is suspected to be small.

An additional economic inefficiency arises if vendors change location to avoid collecting sales taxes. The location change would likely result in higher transportation costs. In the long run, it is conceivable that the higher transportation costs would erode the advantage of evading the sales tax.

For example, consider a Virginia consumer who wants to buy a set of woodworking chisels. The local Virginia hardware store sells the set for $50 (including profit). An Internet-savvy hardware store in Georgia is willing to sell the same chisel set for $52 inclusive of profit and shipping costs. So, before taxes, the local retailer could offer the chisels at a lower price. The marginal customer, who is indifferent between the two retailers before taxes (even though the Internet is more expensive, it is more convenient), is therefore just as likely to buy from the Internet retailer as from the local retailer.

Virginia imposes a state and local sales tax of 5.0%, thus yielding a final sales price to the consumer of $52.50. Given the higher relative price inclusive of the tax, the marginal consumer, along with many other consumers, would likely switch to buying chisels from the Georgia-based Internet retailer (assuming these consumers do not feel compelled to pay the required Virginia use tax on the Internet purchase). The diversion from retail to the Internet in response to the non-collection of the use tax represents a loss in economic efficiency. The additional $2 in production costs ($52 less $50) represents the efficiency loss to society from evading the use tax.

Note that in the absence of sales and use taxes, the Internet vendor in the above example may yield to market forces and close up shop. However, if the Internet vendor continues to operate even without the tax advantage, it could be the case that consumers are willing to pay higher prices for the convenience of Internet shopping. If this were true, then the higher "production costs" for Internet vendors would not necessarily result in an efficiency loss.

Equity

The sales tax is often criticized as a regressive tax—a tax that disproportionately burdens the poor. Assuming Internet shoppers are relatively better off and do not remit use taxes as prescribed by state law, they can avoid paying tax on a larger portion of their consumption expenditures than those without Internet access at home or work. Consumers without ready Internet access are not afforded the same opportunity to "evade" the sales and use tax. In this way, electronic commerce may arguably exacerbate the regressiveness of the sales tax, at least in the short run. As computers and access to the Internet become more readily available, the potential inequity arising from this aspect of the "digital divide" could diminish.

Equity issues also arise with respect to businesses. Currently, local retailers are required to collect sales taxes for the state at the point of sale. Internet retailers, in contrast, are not faced with that administrative burden. Thus, two otherwise equal retailers face different state and local tax burdens. In relatively high tax rate states, this disparity may be significant. As noted earlier, consumers in these high tax rate states have a greater incentive to purchase from out-of-state vendors, exacerbating the tax burden differential.

Differential Effect among States

The growth of Internet-based commerce will have the greatest effect on the states most reliant on the sales and use tax. In addition to having more revenue at risk, high reliance states also face greater efficiency losses because of their generally higher state tax rates. As noted above, higher rates drive a larger wedge between the retail price inclusive of the sales tax and the Internet price and thus exacerbate the efficiency loss from the sales tax. States with low rates (and less reliance) would tend to have a smaller wedge between the two modes of transaction. States with both a high rate and high reliance would tend to recognize the greatest revenue loss from a ban on the taxation of Internet transactions.

Revenue Loss Estimates

Researchers estimated in April 2009 that total state and local revenue loss from "new e-commerce" in 2012 will be approximately $11.4 billion.[15] "New e-commerce" is the lost revenue from states not collecting the use tax on remote Internet transactions. This estimate excludes purchases made over the telephone or through catalogs that would have occurred anyway. California is projected to lose $1.9 billion; Texas, $870.4 million; and New York, $865.5 million.

End Notes

[1] Donald Bruce, William F. Fox, LeAnn Luna, "State and Local Government Sales Tax Revenue Losses From Electronic Commerce," *State Tax Notes*, 52(7):537-558, May 18, 2009, p. 7. Version available at University of Tennessee Center for Business and Economic Research, http://cber.bus.utk.edu/ecomm.htm.

[2] Federation of Tax Administrators, State Sales Tax Rates and Food and Drug Exemptions, January 1, 2011, available at http://www.taxadmin.org/fta/rate/sales.pdf. In three additional states, groceries are subject to local sales taxes only.

[3] A common identity in economics is: income = consumption + saving. The sales tax is a tax on consumption.

[4] Bruce, Donald, William F. Fox, LeAnn Luna, "State and Local Government Sales Tax Revenue Losses From Electronic Commerce," *State Tax Notes*, 52(7):537-558, May 18, 2009. Version available at University of Tennessee Center for Business and Economic Research, http://cber.bus.utk.edu/ecomm.htm.

[5] New Hampshire and Tennessee levy a tax on income from dividends and interest.

[6] For the latest update, see http://www.streamlinedsalestax.org.

[7] SSUTA, Section 102: Fundamental Purpose, p. 7.

[8] For a discussion of the theoretical deficiencies U.S. sales and use tax administration, see Walter Hellerstein and Charles E. McLure Jr., "Sales Taxation of Electronic Commerce: What John Due Knew All Along," *State Tax Notes*, January 1, 2001, pp. 41-46.

[9] Streamlined Sales Tax Project, SSUTA, p. 13.

[10] National Governor's Association, *Policy Position EDC-10: Streamlining State Sales Tax Systems*, February 28, 2011, effective through Winter Meetings 2013, available at http://www.nga.org/portal/site/nga/menuitem.b14a675ba7f89cf9e8ebb856a11010a0.

[11] S. 1832 would also grant SSUTA member states the authority to compel out-of-state vendors in member states to collect sales and use taxes, but, importantly would also provide for an alternative for non-member states. S. 1832 is explained in more detail in the next section.

[12] The American Independent Business Alliance, an advocacy group supporting the collection of sales taxes on Amazon sales, identified these states. The information is available at http://www.amiba.net/resources/news-archive/amazon-nexus-subsidiaries.

[13] Other states with an "Amazon Law" include Illinois, Rhode Island, and North Carolina. For more see Steele, Thomas H., Andres Vallejo, and Kirsten Wolff, "No Solicitations: The 'Amazon' Laws And the Perils of Affiliate Advertising," *State Tax Notes*, March 28, 2011, pp. 939- 944.

[14] See the testimony of Paul Misener, Vice President of World-Wide Public Policy, Amazon.com, Inc. before the U.S. Congress, House Committee on the Judiciary, *Constitutional Limitations on States' Authority to Collect Sales Taxes in E-Commerce*, 112th Cong., 1st sess., November 30, 2011.

[15] Bruce, Donald, William F. Fox, and LeAnn Luna, "State and Local Government Sales Tax Revenue Losses from Electronic Commerce," *State Tax Notes*, 52(7):537-558, May 18, 2009. Version available at University of Tennessee Center for Business and Economic Research, http://cber.bus.utk.edu/ecomm.htm.

In: Taxation of Internet Sales ISBN: 978-1-62257-974-7
Editors: Keith Joyner and Carl Sawhill © 2013 Nova Science Publishers, Inc.

Chapter 3

STATEMENT OF HOUSE JUDICIARY COMMITTEE CHAIRMAN LAMAR SMITH. HEARING ON "CONSTITUTIONAL LIMITATIONS ON STATES' AUTHORITY TO COLLECT SALES TAXES IN E-COMMERCE"[*]

The Constitution grants Congress the exclusive power to regulate interstate commerce. By negative inference, a state may not unduly burden interstate commerce—a constitutional principle commonly referred to as the "dormant commerce clause."

As applied to state tax policy, the dormant commerce clause prohibits a state from taxing a person with whom it lacks a "substantial nexus." In tax terminology, "nexus" refers to the relationship between the taxing authority and the taxpayer.

In its 1992 decision in *Quill Corporation vs. North Dakota*, 19 years ago, the Supreme Court held that, at least for purposes of collecting sales tax, a state lacks substantial nexus over a taxpayer that has no physical presence in the state. The *Quill* court thus established a bright-line physical presence rule for sales tax nexus.

In the *Quill* Decision, the Supreme Court was concerned with burdens to America's small businesses. It reasoned that without a bright-line physical presence rule for nexus, thousands of state and local taxing jurisdictions across America—each with their own unique tax bases and rates—would use vague

---

[*] This is an edited, reformatted and augmented version of the testimony given on November 30, 2011 before the House Judiciary Committee.

concepts like "economic nexus" to impose sales tax collection requirements on businesses.

In the courts view, uncertainty about what jurisdiction has power to tax, as well as compliance with numerous and difficult tax policies, would place an undue burden on interstate commerce.

Today we will hear testimony from online retailers, brick-and-mortar retailers, and state governments about the impact of *Quill* on their operations.

This hearing will explore two issues: First, whether Congress should exercise its Commerce Clause power to enact sales tax reform legislation. And second, if Congress should act, how we can do so in a manner that does not increase administrative and compliance burdens on America's small businesses.

Some in the online retail community believe that physical presence is a fine rule for sales tax nexus. Online retailers typically maintain physical presence in only a handful of states and rely on common carriers to transport purchased goods to customers.

Most states therefore cannot require those online retailers to collect and remit sales tax. Some argue that shielding businesses from the complex patchwork of sales tax laws was precisely the benefit of *Quill* and that Congress should take no action.

But it is precisely this reality that frustrates brick-and-mortar retailers, who claim to suffer a competitive disadvantage compared to their online counterparts.

State revenues are also affected by the *Quill* rule. Forty-five states and the District of Columbia have a sales tax. Those jurisdictions also have a "use" tax, equal to the sales tax rate, which residents must pay for the usage, consumption or storage of goods purchased in a non-resident state and brought into the resident state.

For example, a shopper in Austin, Texas who buys goods online from a retailer that lacks a physical presence in Texas is responsible to pay Texas use tax even though he pays no sales tax on his transaction.

But states rely on taxpayers to self-report their purchases in other states, and states lack the resources and means to effectively police use tax avoidance. So online purchases usually escape taxation altogether.

Some believe that Congress should not come to the states' assistance—if a state chooses to impose a use tax, it should also find a way to enforce it. Others would like to see Congress help states collect sales taxes on all transactions, thereby eliminating the need for use taxes.

In: Taxation of Internet Sales   ISBN: 978-1-62257-974-7
Editors: Keith Joyner and Carl Sawhill   © 2013 Nova Science Publishers, Inc.

Chapter 4

TESTIMONY OF DAN MARSHALL, OWNER, MARSHALL MUSIC CO. HEARING ON "CONSTITUTIONAL LIMITATIONS ON STATES' AUTHORITY TO COLLECT SALES TAXES IN E-COMMERCE"[*]

Good morning Chairman Smith, Ranking Member Conyers, and members of the Committee. My name is Dan Marshall, a small business owner from Lansing, Michigan, and I appreciate this opportunity to testify before the Committee this morning on leveling the playing field for Main Street. I am testifying today on behalf of the Michigan Retailers Association and the millions of Main Street merchants throughout the U.S.

I am the 2nd generation operator of a family-owned chain of music stores called Marshall Music, with seven bricks-and-mortar stores located throughout Michigan. My mother and father founded Marshall Music in 1948 and over the last 63 years the company has grown into the mid-west's largest retailer of band and orchestra instruments. We are an integral part of the community providing jobs, job training, paying property taxes, and even providing a service to the state by collecting and remitting sales taxes. Without businesses like mine, there would be no Main Street.

We proudly employ 300 full time and part time employees, down approximately 10 percent from our peak a few years ago. Sales volume has been as high as $24 million and last year we did around $18.5 million in sales

---

[*] This is an edited, reformatted and augmented version of the testimony given on November 30, 2011 before the House Judiciary Committee.

through our seven store fronts, and around 5 years ago we started selling some items online through eBay averaging $125,000 annually.

For the last 63 years, Marshall Music has operated across the state serving musicians, schools, students, teachers, enthusiasts and more. We sell music instruments, equipment, and offer performance space and lessons to shoppers and musicians. We pride ourselves on customer service and having knowledgeable associates who can help match shoppers with the right products.

I do not have to tell you that retail is a fiercely competitive industry. As we are now in one of the busiest shopping seasons of the year, we are – *and must* – stay price competitive with the guys not just down the street, but also our competitors online. But that competition is no longer on a level playing field, and the business my mother and father started is facing an unprecedented attack they never could have envisioned 60 years ago.

Today, bricks-and-mortar stores like ours are becoming the showrooms for online-only companies like Overstock, Amazon and eBay. Customers literally come into our stores every single day to play, touch, look at, and evaluate higher-end musical equipment, only to walk out of the store and go home to purchase the item from an online retailer that does not collect the state sales tax at the point of purchase.

Retailers have always had the ability to match prices. For the professional music equipment Marshall Music sells, our customers are very sophisticated on price. Our sales associates are fully aware of online prices and we are able to match those prices for customers. Matching or beating the price of a competitor – regardless of whether it is a bricks-and-mortar store or an online shop – is part of retail. Always has been and always will be. But what I cannot do is tell the customer that I do not have to charge them the state sales tax. In fact, if I did that, I'd find myself audited, fined and potentially thrown in jail.

And for those customers that are convinced they are getting a special deal when the sales tax is not collected by an online retailer, most are completely unaware that they still owe the state sales tax on that item regardless of whether they purchased the item in my store or online. But when I collect it at the register I do a service for the both the state and the customer, relieving the latter of the burden of collecting receipts and calculating their sales tax – something they are legally required (but rarely do) for online purchases.

A recent national survey found that three-quarters of consumers were not even aware they had this obligation when filing state tax returns. This same survey found that sixty-one percent of consumers, when informed of their obligations, support Congress passing legislation that would allow states to require online-only retailers to collect state sales tax just like storefronts in the community.

Back home in Michigan we have a state sales tax of 6 percent that is tacked onto every purchase. These are funds that states use to keep our schools running and to make sure our communities stay safe. As a small business owner I would be happy if there was not a sales tax in the state, but I know that is not necessarily practical. But if we are going to pay for essential services with a sales tax, I want everybody to play by the same rules. Regardless of whether a sale occurs in a store or online, the sales tax should be the same. In a free market, government should not be giving one type of business an advantage over everyone else.

Make no mistake; I am not afraid of online competition. As I mentioned earlier in my testimony, I do sell a small number of items through eBay, and I welcome the technological advances that have enabled me to do that. But at the same time, the internet is no longer in its infancy, and it makes little sense to continue to give online sellers special treatment in the tax code to the detriment of everyone else. In fact, I would gladly collect sales taxes for the out-of-state sales I make on eBay if it meant a level playing field for everyone. The reality is that software exists today to make the calculation quite simple – it is no longer the burden it was 20 years ago, and giant online retailers like Overstock, Amazon and eBay know it.

The bottom line is that a sale, is a sale, is a sale, regardless of how the item was purchased.

To be clear, fixing this problem is **not** imposing a new tax on anyone. Forcing an online-only retailer to collect owed sales taxes is not a new tax on that online business: it is simply having them play by the same rules as bricks-and-mortar businesses who already collect on behalf of their customers.

In the past decade, this is a problem that has manifested into a direct threat to jobs on Main Street. Online commerce has been growing at a rate of over 10 percent annually, and it will only continue to sharply rise. We simply cannot compete when the government gives an unfair advantage to one segment of the retail community. Stores will continue to close down and jobs will continue to be lost in our communities until Congress closes this loophole and creates a level playing field.

Earlier this year the Michigan Retailers Association released a study that found that up to 1,600 new jobs would be created in our state if Congress took action. I am troubled that some view this issue as a tax increase – nothing could be further from the truth. This is a collection and fairness issue and it is time to close this loophole and in doing so it will help states like mine avoid the potential of raising other taxes. As I understand it, several states are considering opportunities to use any new revenues from closing this loophole to reduce the overall in-state tax burden. This would be something that all business owners would applaud.

So I am here today asking Congress to pass a national solution that levels the playing field between bricks-and-mortar stores and online-only companies. I am asking that you do this not only for Marshall Music, but for every single book store, bicycle store and local jewelry store back in your district.

While I am aware this is an oversight hearing, I do note it is within the purview of Congress to fix this problem and protect Main Street jobs. Because of the effect of a 1992 Supreme Court decision (Quill vs. North Dakota), states alone cannot solve this problem. A number of states – California, Texas, Illinois, and South Carolina, to name a few – have recently passed state laws that deal with the unfair treatment between online-only and bricks-and-mortar retailers. The Quill decision, however, limits how far states can go. It is clearly time for, and the responsibility of, Congress to address this at a national level and provide a solution to protect jobs in each of your districts.

In particular, I note that a bipartisan bill, H.R. 3179, the Marketplace Equity Act, gives every state the option to fix this issue. H.R. 3179 allows the 24 states that belong to the Streamlined Sales and Use Tax Agreement to level the playing field. As well, H.R. 3179 gives simple options to the remaining 21 states that are not party to, and many never join, the Streamlined Sales and Use Tax Agreement in order to begin treating all retailers equally. The legislation is a breakthrough in that it supports the rights of individual states to determine what is the best way for them to solve this problem. H.R. 3179 is also supported by a broad range of national associations, state retail organizations, and companies. I have attached a copy of their letter of support to my testimony and would ask that it be submitted for the record.

In closing, I want to thank the Committee for providing me this opportunity to appear before you this morning. Main Street merchants are asking Congress to close this loophole and give us a level playing field to compete on.

I look forward to answering any questions you may have.

November 2, 2011

The Honorable Patty Murray
Co-Chair, Joint Select Committee on Deficit Reduction
U.S. Senate

Washington, DC 20510

The Honorable Jeb Hensarling
Co-Chair, Joint Select Committee on Deficit Reduction
U. S. House of Representatives
Washington, DC 20515

Dear Senator Murray and Representative Hensarling:

The undersigned companies and state and national trade associations write today to ask that you include in your recommendations to the House and Senate a provision that would close a loophole harming traditional bricks-and-mortar retail businesses while assisting the states in collecting approximately $23 billion in uncollected state sales taxes that are currently due on Internet and catalogue sales.

At issue is a decades-old Supreme Court ruling, which was issued in 1992, before the pervasiveness of today's Internet commerce, and which prohibits states from requiring remote sellers to collect sales and use taxes owed on purchases from out-of-state vendors. This loophole has created an uneven playing field for bricks-and-mortar retail businesses that face a price disadvantage, has led to budget shortfalls for states as sales taxes go uncollected, and an undue burden on consumers who do not realize they owe the sales tax if it is not collected by the seller, leaving them to face penalties and increased scrutiny from state auditors. Main street retailers are jeopardized as a result of the insurmountable price disadvantage created by this government subsidy along with 15 million bricks-and-mortar retail jobs and one in 10 jobs related to shopping centers. Recent data suggests that one in four jobs is directly or indirectly related to the retail sector.

Several bills are pending in the House and Senate that would give states the authority to manage their sales tax laws while closing this loophole. H.R. 3179, the Marketplace Equity Act, introduced by Reps. Steve Womack (R-AR) and Jackie Speier (D-CA) provides an option for every state to simplify its sales tax statute and assist vendors with compliance, while providing for a robust small business exemption.

S. 1452 and H.R. 2701, the Main Street Fairness Act, introduced by Sen. Dick Durbin (D-IL) and Rep. John Conyers (D-MI) would sanction a 24-state compact called the Streamlined Sales and Use Tax Agreement, providing these states with authority to require collection on remote sales. Senators Durbin, Enzi, and Alexander are also working on a bi-partisan solution, the

Marketplace Fairness Act. While all these bills generally accomplish the same goal, they have one item in common: only Congress can grant this authority to the states.

As you seek solutions to address the federal budget, any final product will undoubtedly have an impact on the states, which are likewise facing their own budget crises. Consistent with the goals of the Joint Select Committee on Deficit Reduction, Congress has an opportunity to help the states resolve their own budget shortfalls by enhancing states' rights over sales tax collection authority and in the process closing a loophole that will level the playing field for all merchants. The Joint Select Committee on Deficit Reduction can easily include this authority in its recommendations to the full House and Senate, and we urge you to do so.

Sincerely,

NATIONAL TRADE ASSOCIATIONS

American Booksellers Association
American Specialty Toy Retailing Association
American Veterinary Medical Association
Association for Christian Retail
Food Marketing Institute
Independent Running Retailer Association
International Council of Shopping Centers
National Association of Chain Drug Stores
National Association of College Stores
National Association of Real Estate Investment Trusts
National Bicycle Dealers Association
National Grocers Association
National Home Furnishings Association
National Retail Federation
North American Retail Dealers Association
Outdoor Industry Association (OIA)
Pet Industry Joint Advisory Council
Professional Beauty Association
Real Estate Roundtable
Retail Industry Leaders Association
Soccer Dealer Association

STATE TRADE ASSOCIATIONS

Alabama Retail Association
Alliance of Wisconsin Retailers
Arizona Retailers Association
Arkansas Grocers and Retail Merchants Association
California Business Properties Association
California Retailers Association
Carolinas Food Industry Council
Colorado Retail Council
Connecticut Retail Merchants Association
Florida Retail Federation
Georgia Retail Association
Idaho Retailers Association
Illinois Retail Merchants Association
Indiana Retail Council
Iowa Retail Federation
Kentucky Retail Federation
Los Angeles Area Chamber of Commerce
Louisiana Retailers Association
Maryland Retailers Association
Michigan Retailers Association
Minnesota Retail Association
Missouri Retailers Association
Mountains and Plains Independent Booksellers Association
Nebraska Retail Federation
New Atlantic Independent Booksellers Association
New England Independent Booksellers Association
New Jersey Retail Merchants Association
North Carolina Retail Merchants Association
North Dakota Retail Association
Ohio Council of Retail Merchants
Pacific Northwest Booksellers Association
Pennsylvania Retailers' Association
Retail Association of Mississippi
Retail Association of Nevada
Retail Council of New York State
Retail Merchants of Hawaii
Retailers Association of Massachusetts

Rhode Island Retail Federation
South Carolina Retail Merchants Association
South Dakota Retailers Association
Southern Independent Booksellers Alliance
Tennessee Retail Association
Texas Retailers Association
Utah Food Industry Association
Utah Retail Merchants Association
Vermont Retail Association
Virginia Retail Merchants Association
Washington Retail Association
West Virginia Retailers Association
Wyoming Retail Association

COMPANIES

Abbell Credit Corporation, Chicago, IL
Acadia Realty Trust, White Plains, NY
AutoZone
Barnes and Noble
Bed, Bath, & Beyond
Best Buy
Blake Hunt Ventures, Inc., Danville, CA
John Bucksbaum, Private Real Estate Investor/Developer, Former Chairman and CEO of General Growth Properties, Inc., Chicago, IL
Build-A-Bear Workshop®, Saint Louis, MO
CBL & Associates Properties, Inc., Chattanooga, TN
Cencor Realty Services, Dallas, TX
Chesterfield Blue Valley, LLC, St. Louis, MO
The Container Store, Dallas, Texas
The CortiGilchrist Partnership, llc, Al Corti, Principal, San Diego, CA
Dick's Sporting Goods
DDR Corp., Beachwood, OH
DLC Management Corp., Tarrytown, NY
Donahue Schriber Realty Group, Costa Mesa, CA
Edens & Avant, Columbia, SC
Evergreen Devco, Inc., Glendale, CA
Fairfield Corporation, Battle Creek, MI

Federal Realty Investment Trust, Rockville, MD
FedTax, David Campbell, CEO
L. Michael Foley and Associates, LLC, La Jolla, CA
Forest City Enterprises, Inc., Cleveland, OH
Gap Inc., San Francisco, CA
Garrison Pacific Properties, San Rafael, CA
General Growth Properties, Chicago, IL
Glimcher Realty Trust, Columbus, OH
The Greeby Companies, Inc., Chicago, IL
Hart Realty Advisers, Inc., Simsbury, CT
David Hocker & Associates, Inc., Owensboro, Kentucky
D. Talmage Hocker, The Hocker Group, Louisville, KY
Kimco Realty Corporation, New Hyde Park, NY
Limited Brands, Columbus OH
Lowes
Malcolm Riley and Associates Los Angeles, CA
Mary Lou Fiala, CEO, Loft Unlimited, Ponte Vedra Beach Florida
Marketing Developments, Inc. MI
Planning Developments, Inc. MI
JC Penney
Petco
The Pratt Company, Mill Valley, CA
The Rappaport Companies, McLean, VA
REI (Recreational Equipment, Inc.)
Reininga Corporation, Healdsburg, CA
Safeway, Inc.
Sears Holdings
The Seayco Group, Bentonville, AK
The Sembler Company, St. Petersburg, FL
Simon Property Group, Indianapolis, IN
Steiner + Associates LLC, Columbus, Ohio
Stirling Properties, Covington, LA
Tanger Factory Outlet Centers, Inc., Greensboro, NC
Target Corporation, Minneapolis, MN
Taubman Realty Group, Bloomfield Hills, MI
Tractor Supply Company
Vestar Development Co. - Phoenix AZ
Wal-Mart Stores, Bentonville, AR
The Weitzman Group, Dallas, Texas

Western Development Corporation, Washington, DC
Westfield, LLC., Los Angeles, CA
WDP Partners, LLC, Phoenix, AZ
Wolfe Properties, LLC, St. Louis, MO

In: Taxation of Internet Sales   ISBN: 978-1-62257-974-7
Editors: Keith Joyner and Carl Sawhill © 2013 Nova Science Publishers, Inc.

Chapter 5

TESTIMONY OF DR. PATRICK M. BYRNE, CHAIRMAN AND CEO, OVERSTOCK.COM, INC. HEARING ON "CONSTITUTIONAL LIMITATIONS ON STATES' AUTHORITY TO COLLECT SALES TAXES IN E-COMMERCE"[*]

Chairman Smith and Members of the Committee,

My name is Dr. Patrick M. Byrne. I am the Chairman and CEO of Overstock.com, Inc., an E-commerce retailer which last year had 1,500 employees, $1.1 billion in revenue and $14 million in net income. Thank you for the invitation to testify today as the Committee explores the constitutional limitations on states' authority to impose sales tax collection obligations on non-resident E-commerce retailers like Overstock. I have views on this subject because, from my experience, I believe that if the proposed collection obligations had existed in October 1999 when Overstock.com launched, we would likely not be here today. The odds against a new online business being successful are long in any case, but requiring online businesses to collect sales tax on behalf of remote state governments without remuneration, simplification and indemnity, make those odds even slimmer. So I appreciate this opportunity to share my views on this subject.

---

[*] This is an edited, reformatted and augmented version of the testimony given on November 30, 2011 before the House Judiciary Committee.

About Overstock

Overstock is a publicly traded Utah-based Internet retailer that launched in 1999 with 18 employees and $1.8 million in sales. In 2010, Overstock had 1,500 employees, all in Utah, $1.1 billion of revenues, and $14 million of net income. We offer a wide variety of high-quality, brand-name merchandise and services at discount prices, including bedding, home decor, appliances, watches, jewelry, electronics, sporting goods, clothing, shoes, cars, vacations and insurance. We give customers an opportunity to shop for bargains conveniently, while offering manufacturers, distributors and other retailers an alternative sales channel.

In 1999, we offered less than 100 products for sale; today the number is about 1 million. For each of the last six years, various industry groups, including the National Retail Federation and American Express, have routinely ranked Overstock as #1, 2, 3, or 4 in customer satisfaction among all U.S. retailers, online and off. In 2010, Forbes ranked Overstock as the number one retailer in employee satisfaction, and Glassdoor ranked Overstock ninth in its list of top 50 corporations in America to work.

We have long been noted for our corporate social responsibility. In 2001, we launched Worldstock Fair Trade, Overstock's socially responsible store for products handcrafted by artisans from developing nations and rural areas of the USA. The department distinguishes itself from its competitors by returning between 60-70% of the sales price to the artisans. To date, we have returned more than $73 million to Worldstock's artisan suppliers. We donate all profits from Worldstock to charity, and we use most to build schools and orphanages in some of the poorest nations in the world. For us to be here today, my colleagues at Overstock have had to be fanatics about service, adaptation, and innovation.

The Burden of Remote State Sales Tax Collection

The question the Committee must consider is whether innovative remote sale companies will emerge, employ Americans, and help our economy grow if Congress alters the status quo by allowing states to burden interstate commerce. In my opinion, the pending bills allow states to shirk *their* responsibility to administer and collect the taxes *they* impose on the taxable "end consumer." Instead, they pass that burden on to non-resident, non-voting businesses. Passage of such legislation would curtail the emergence of the next innovative E-commerce company and poison the Internet's fertile ground for growth and innovation.

Overstock is physically present only in Utah. All of our operations, servers, and employees are located in Utah. As I have already indicated, if when we launched in 1999 and had only $1.8 million of revenue, we had been required in states in which we had no presence to calculate and collect sales tax in thousands of separate taxing districts, respecting their thousands of unique taxing practices and tax holidays, we would not have survived to grow and provide the 1,500 jobs we now do. The cost of compliance in what is currently reported as 9,746 taxing jurisdictions, the unavailability—even today—of affordable off-the-shelf plug-and-play software solutions, the cost of employing and training people to implement and run the software, the administration and resolution of state audits and resulting assessments, and the risk of penalties and suits by plaintiff bar attorneys for software errors and omissions, would have been too high a hurdle to overcome. I imagine the same could be said for Newegg, Amazon, eBay and other E-commerce start-up companies that have blossomed over the last decade.

We oppose the pending bills because they "outsource" to retailers, without compensation, the burden of collecting taxes from residents of states where those retailers have no physical presence nexus. The absence of a physical presence nexus requirement, the long-standing Constitutional standard to be met before states may impose burdens of taxation beyond their borders, makes remote sales tax collection a burden on innovation, entry, and commerce. The taxing jurisdiction should be primarily, if not exclusively, responsible for collecting sales tax from its residents. If states want or need to hire retailers to collect sales taxes from their residents, true "fairness" requires that the states provide them with: (1) plug-and-play software solutions, (2) indemnification from computation, collection, and administration errors, and (3) compensation for doing the tax collection work on behalf of those states.

WHY NEXUS IS CRITICAL

It is unfair to allow states the ability to impose collection obligations on remote E-commerce retailers that have no physical nexus with the state. Imposing such an obligation on a company that has no political say in the taxing decision, the election of state and local officials who make that decision, or how the tax revenues are used, is about as perfect a definition of taxation without representation as can be devised in the 21st Century.

For a remote seller, determining what transactions are taxable and at what rate in a given jurisdiction is extremely complex. For example, we sell gift baskets. Some of the nearly 10,000 taxing jurisdictions impose sales tax on the entire basket of goods, others exempt food products from taxation, and others treat some of the products as candy subject to a higher tax. I trust you see the problem. Back-to-school sales tax holidays for clothes and supplies are another example. It is far easier for retailers with a physical presence in a jurisdiction to know the tax nuances of their jurisdiction. But it is vastly more complex for an E-commerce retailer with thousands or millions of products to know the specifics of the nearly 10,000 taxing authorities where they are not physically present. Thus, if Congress allows states to shift the sales tax collection obligation to retailers, it must require that states supply the software solution. Failure to do so exacerbates the heavy burden to entry of startups and small businesses.

THE STATUS QUO IS A SUCCESS

In *Quill Corp. v. North Dakota,* 504 U.S. 298 (1992), the U. S. Supreme Court articulated a bright-line physical presence requirement before North Dakota could impose a collection burden on an out-of-state mail order business (a business model nearly identical to online retailers). The Court stated:

> Moreover, a bright-line rule in the area of sales and use taxes also encourages settled expectations and, in doing so, fosters investment by businesses and individuals. Indeed, it is not unlikely that the mail-order industry's dramatic growth over the last quarter-century is due in part to the bright-line exemption from state taxation created in *Bellas Hess.*

The physical presence standard of *Quill* has worked successfully, enabling technology companies like Overstock to innovate and thrive in the retail marketplace, bring unprecedented value, choice and convenience to consumers, and enable small retail stores throughout the country to supplement their sales through our web sites.

A FAIRER APPROACH IF A FEDERAL SOLUTION IS ESSENTIAL

Given these benefits, it is difficult for me to understand why Congress would pass legislation that creates insurmountable hurdles for new entrants and ideas. If, nevertheless, a majority in Congress wants to upset the status quo, Overstock believes that a fair legislative package must include the following elements.

1. First, because tax collection is really a duty of states and not retailers, the states should be required to provide a truly plug-and-play affordable software solution. Proponents of the pending legislation say such solutions are readily available in the marketplace, so this should not be a problem. The truth is, however, that they are not. I speak from recent experience at Overstock. We have been considering creating nexus in the state of Kentucky. In preparation for that event, we acquired what was described as an affordable plug-and-play software package that would ensure we were in compliance with the sales tax collection obligations for online sales to residents of the new jurisdiction. The off-the-shelf software required approximately $300,000 of investment and months of man-hours of our IT staff to build. Implementation of this solution for the nation's nearly 10,000 different taxing jurisdictions would be extraordinarily costly for companies like ours. So if states want to tax our sales to their residents when we have no physical presence there, they should bear the cost of supplying the software.

2. Second, we should not be held liable to the states or to plaintiff law suits if errors arise from use of software solutions they provide, like missing a tax holiday, or a new tax rate, or the fact that one city in the state taxes candy while another does not.

3. Third, taxing authorities should compensate all retailers whom they require to collect sales taxes. There are significant costs associated with collecting and remitting the tax to the jurisdiction. Just as I cannot force my colleagues to work for free, states should not be allowed, in essence, to force-hire companies to do their work without expense reimbursement and some degree of revenue sharing.

In the event that Congress opts to end the status quo in favor of a federal solution for sales tax collection, Overstock has prepared the attached draft bill incorporating the principles that I have outlined. We believe that it should garner the support of the majority of E-commerce companies, as well as many bricks and mortar and bricks and clicks retailers, particularly smaller and mid-sized main street retailers who are otherwise hurt by the currently proposed bills.

CONCLUSION

Thank you, Chairman Smith, for inviting me to share Overstock.com's views on the sales tax issue. I truly appreciate this opportunity. I would be pleased to answer any questions you or Members of the Committee have. Overstock is eager to remain engaged in this debate.

In: Taxation of Internet Sales   ISBN: 978-1-62257-974-7
Editors: Keith Joyner and Carl Sawhill   © 2013 Nova Science Publishers, Inc.

Chapter 6

TESTIMONY OF JOHN OTTO, REPRESENTATIVE, TEXAS HOUSE OF REPRESENTATIVES. HEARING ON "CONSTITUTIONAL LIMITATIONS ON STATES' AUTHORITY TO COLLECT SALES TAXES IN E-COMMERCE"*

Mr. Chairman and members of the committee, thank you for the opportunity to testify today regarding the issue of Constitutional Limitations on States' Authority to Collect Sales Taxes in E-Commerce. My name is John Otto. I am a certified public accountant serving my fourth term in the Texas House of Representatives, where I serve as vice-chairman of the Committee on Ways and Means and as a subcommittee chair on the House Appropriations Committee. I am employed by Ryan, a tax advisory and consulting firm with the largest indirect tax practice in North America. I am pleased today to testify in my capacity as a State Representative.

During the 82nd Legislative Session in Texas this year, I carried legislation to more clearly define the nexus statutes and physical presence. My changes were somewhat conservative compared to what other states were attempting in that I did not include "affiliated marketers" as establishing nexus in Texas, but did address a retailer (including any 50% or more controlled affiliated entity) who had physical presence by means other than a retail store front. The definition included "distribution centers" specifically as constituting physical

---

* This is an edited, reformatted and augmented version of the testimony given on November 30, 2011 before the House Judiciary Committee.

presence. The legislation was supported by 125 of 150 House members and 30 of 31 Senators. Each state is reacting to the current market place in its own way, but we are constrained at the end of the day by the *Quill* decision.

In 1992, the U.S. Supreme Court opined in *Quill Corp. v. North Dakota* that a retailer does not have an obligation to collect sales tax if they have no "physical presence." Since then, the *Quill* decision has been the law of the land and "physical presence" has been the measuring stick for whether or not a retailer has to collect sales tax. Quoting from the Supreme Court's decision in *Quill* regarding the reasons the justices disagreed with the North Dakota Supreme Court's decision **"This aspect of our decision is made easier by the fact that the underlying issue is not only one that Congress may be better qualified to resolve, but also one that Congress has the ultimate power to resolve."** I believe this opinion shows that the ball is in your court.

Over the last 19 years technology has advanced in the marketplace to the point that physical presence can largely be controlled and isolated to a few states while selling into many states. If action is not taken and *Quill* is allowed to remain the law of the land, then are we not picking winners and losers within the retail sector? How is a retailer, such as Bed, Bath and Beyond, J.C. Penny or Wai-Mart supposed to compete with Amazon.com, Blue Nile.com or Overtstocked.com when the latter enjoy anywhere from an 8-10% discount due to not having to collect sales tax. And all of the companies I have listed as storefront retailers also conduct sales over the internet and currently collect tax on those sales. This current law and policy discourages the continued development of the very brick and mortar establishments that support our state and local communities in numerous ways. This issue of fairness should be addressed and I believe that **H.R.** 3179 does that.

H.R. 3179, in my opinion, levels the playing field while protecting states' rights. Previous legislation that has been introduced in Congress has contained the requirement that a state join the Streamlined Sales Tax compact in order to receive the benefits of that legislation. While I fully support the rights of states to join the compact, I do not believe a state should be forced into joining the compact in order to receive the benefit of such legislation. As astate representative I am not willing to turn over to an unelected, nonpolitical body the right to determine what items will be subject to sales and use tax within my state. **H.R.** 3179 leaves it up to each state whether they wish to join the compact or not. Let me also point out that in my opinion the Streamlined states will comply with the requirements of **H.R.** 3179 as soon as they adopt a small business exemption. So they are at a distinct advantage in regards to how quickly they can implement H.R. 3179.

The provisions of **H.R.** 3179 basically have four minimum requirements for a state to avail itself of the benefits provided in this legislation:

1. Small business exemption
2. Uniform tax base rules within a state-what is and is not taxable
3. Centralized filing and remitting within a state
4. Tax rates: Either
   - State rate only (not local)
   - Blended rate -state and partial local rates
   - Address-based rate with software made available

In my opinion the requirement for a uniform tax base within a state (which is desirable) may cause delays in implementing the provisions of **H.R.** 3179 for some states, unless the tax rate options are included in the final legislation. In Texas, locals may tax residential electricity and may not impose tax on interstate telecommunications services and satellite television services. Some other states may have similar situations in which locals may impose their tax on something the state does not (example: Chicago's tax of soft drink cans).

Also, some states permit locals to "opt out" of sales tax holidays and this proposal would appear to preclude that. One solution, to all of the issues just discussed, is for a state to adopt the state only rate or blended rate and have it apply to the state definitions of what is taxable. Because H.R. 3179 requires uniform tax base rules, this needs to be clarified in the final legislation that the uniformity of state and local would only apply should the state choose an address based rate with software made available. The bill also states that local taxing jurisdictions cannot require remote sellers to file returns which may affect states like California, Arizona, Louisiana and Colorado, unless they adopt the state rate only or blended rate. I cannot overemphasize how important I believe it is that the final legislation include all three of the proposed methods of taxation. Adopting the addressed-based rate with software made available as the only method available to states will have a significant impact on which states can participate and how quickly they can comply.

Finally, let me address the revenue side of the equation as it relates to state governments. I know some people will call this a new tax, but it is not. This is a tax that has been due from the consumer, when the retailer is not required to collect it, since sales and use taxes were put into law. Businesses for the most part are already paying the use tax because they are subject to audit if they hold a sales tax permit. With the ever increasing likelihood that states are going to find lesser amounts of federal revenues available to them as you attempt to reduce federal spending, wouldn't it make sense to allow states to have retailers collect a tax that is already in law? Before I vote to increase a state sales tax rate that would only increase the current disparity between local and out of state retailers, it only makes sense to first collect the taxes states are already due. H.R. 3179 helps states accomplish that.

Thank you Mr. Chairman and members of the committee for allowing me to testify today. I would now be happy to answer any questions you might have.

In: Taxation of Internet Sales   ISBN: 978-1-62257-974-7
Editors: Keith Joyner and Carl Sawhill   © 2013 Nova Science Publishers, Inc.

Chapter 7

TESTIMONY OF TOD COHEN, VICE PRESIDENT AND DEPUTY GENERAL COUNSEL, EBAY, INC. HEARING ON "CONSTITUTIONAL LIMITATIONS ON STATES' AUTHORITY TO COLLECT SALES TAXES IN E-COMMERCE"*

Chairman Smith, Ranking Member Conyers, and Members of the Committee: Thank you for the opportunity to testify today about the impact of remote sales tax policies on small businesses that use the eBay platform and the Internet more generally.

My name is Tod Cohen and I am the Vice President of Global Government Relations and Deputy General Counsel for eBay Inc. eBay Inc. was founded in 1995 and is headquartered in San Jose, California. Our business connects millions of buyers and sellers across the globe everyday through the eBay platform, which is the world's largest online marketplace; through PayPal, which enables individuals and businesses to securely, easily and quickly send and receive online payments; and through GSI Commerce, which facilitates e-commerce, multichannel retailing and digital marketing for global enterprises. We also reach millions of consumers through specialized marketplaces such as StubHub, the world's largest ticket marketplace; and eBay Classifieds sites, which together are available in more than 1,000 cities around the world.

---

* This is an edited, reformatted and augmented version of the testimony given on November 30, 2011 before the House Judiciary Committee.

Among those that use the eBay platform are hundreds of thousands of U.S. small businesses and entrepreneurs located in every state and congressional district across the country. The Internet and the eBay marketplace provide these small businesses and entrepreneurs with relatively low-cost access to potential buyers far outside the limits of their traditional geographic footprint. eBay cares about the remote sales tax impacts on these small business retailers and entrepreneurs because they have always been at the heart of the eBay business model. Our success is tied directly to their success. The ability of small business retail to play a meaningful role in the 21st Century retail marketplace is critical for expanding retail competition, developing new businesses and better serving consumers.

Technology and the Internet are now central to almost every retail business model. This is true for small businesses. This is true for mid-size retailers. This is true for retail giants. eBay Inc. is a technology company that enables all size retailers to compete better, but our focus today is on the small business retailers. Internet and mobile technology is critical to their long-term success. By opening up new markets, the Internet empowers small businesses to grow outside of traditionally disadvantaged communities and compete nationwide. eBay and the Internet also open international markets to small business retailers in ways unimaginable just fifteen years ago. In fact, 20% of sales occurring on the eBay platform are cross-border commerce and 90% of small business retailers that use the eBay marketplace export.

Small online businesses provide consumers with greater product selection, competitive prices and convenience. Simply put, more choice for consumers. Especially in this tough economy, consumer choice is more important than ever before.

The debate about remote sales tax policy on the Internet stretches back over a decade. It is basically as old as the commercial Internet itself. While much of the rhetoric fueling the call for increased remote sales tax collection has stood still, the world of retail has changed. Retail businesses, large and small, have fundamentally changed. The very idea that this debate is about "The Internet" v. "Stores" is a false paradigm. All sustainable 21st Century retail business models, large and small alike, use the Internet and other technology tools. All 21st Century retail business models use some physical facilities, whether stores, management offices or distribution centers.

Please look beyond the outdated rhetoric and look at the data, as you consider this issue. First, stores matter and they don't stand alone. They are being combined with technology and web services. The data is unchallenged, most retail still happens in stores. The Census Bureau and Forrester Research shows that in-store retail will represent 93% of all retail in 2012, while online retail is just 7%.[1]

The story of retail competition did not begin with the Internet, as you all know. You also know that the face of retail has changed dramatically over the past four decades. At the heart of the story has been the expanding dominance of giant retailers at the expense of small business. Giants have grown more dominant in retail; small independent retailers have been pushed to the edges. To illustrate, big-box discount retailers accounted for 42% of total retail sales in 1987. As of July 2010, their market share had jumped to 87%.[2] Technology has been part of that story. Today, technology can empower small retailers, and you should support that. At the same time, Internet-based retail is increasingly dominated by giants.

There is a term in the world of 21st Century retail that you should be comfortable using. It is called "Brick & Click" retail. It means a network of stores, web and technology services all combined in a single retail business. Essentially, every large retailer in America operates a "Brick & Click" business. As noted, 93% of retail occurs in stores. Another key data-point is that nearly 45% of those in-store sales are web-influenced.[3] Consumers use their mobile devices and computers to find what they want to buy, locate the store where it is available for the best combination of price and convenience, and they buy it. "Brick & Click" retail is a growing and vibrant retail business model.

The largest "Brick & Click" retailers are the same retail giants that dominate in-store sales. This is not some conspiracy. These are giant and successful retailers that dominated the business in the late 20th Century and they are doing their best to adapt to new technology services and consumer needs. The retail giants make up 18 of the Top 25 retail websites today, and they are trying to use mobile services, social networking and other technologies to better compete.[4] And eBay Inc. is working hard to enable them and almost all other retailers of whatever size to succeed in that effort.

The majority of small business retailers are doing the same thing as their larger competitors, just on a much smaller scale. Like their larger counterparts, small retailers are combining a store, or a few stores, a warehouse, or even their garage, with technology services to try to compete. They face a completely different competitive landscape and cost equation than the giants do. Big and small retailers offer consumers different benefits and their models come with different costs.

The giant billion-dollar retailers with their national stores or distribution networks can offer key services like in-store pick up, same day delivery, free or significantly lower-cost shipping, and in-store returns of items bought online. Consumers value those features, and the biggest of the big are better positioned to offer those services. In retail, being giant has its advantages today just as it did four decades ago. Again, the data does not lie. The largest retailer on the Internet, Amazon, is a business with a national network of facilities, and is growing fastest. The giant "Brick & Click" retailers are also growing their market share online. In short, while small business retailers are active online and are adopting technology, they are not winning the race under the status quo.

The share of online sales being done by retailers with less than $20 million in sales is falling. Under the current mix of business costs, including the remote sales tax rules, the small business competitors are not taking over the field. Instead, it is the largest retailers that are growing. And not surprisingly, those giant retailers are lined up united in proposing a change in remote sales tax law that will harm the smaller retailers who do not have national physical presence. If small business retailers using the Internet were gaining unfair advantages from current remote sales tax laws, one would expect that their share of Internet sales would be growing. But it is not. Just as importantly, the idea that small business retailers on the Internet are a threat to the survival of small business store fronts is ridiculous. The threat to small independent retailers is coming from giant multi-billion dollar competitors online and offline, which has been the case for nearly half a century.

You hear a lot about fairness in this debate. Some have claimed that a "level playing field" means all retailers using the Internet should be held to the same remote sales tax standard. However, sameness is not fairness. Small businesses retailers face many competitive disadvantages when compared to larger retailers. They have proportionally higher costs of doing business, including providing employee benefits. And one must especially consider the costs of shipping, when considering the playing field for small e-commerce businesses,. Shipping prices, as with other costs, are directly related to sales volumes and how close the retailers is to the customer.

Furthermore, customer shopping preferences show that many of the advantages of being a very large retailer are gaining in importance. Again, there are reasons why the largest retailers are growing their share of e-commerce. There are real world benefits to being very big and combining physical assets with online shopping. A recent survey of online shoppers by Kantar Media asked consumers to list services that will encourage them to shop more online. Five of the top six responses are tied directly to having a large physical presence, including in-store returns, in-store pickup and shipping benefits that come from having massive distribution centers near their consumers.

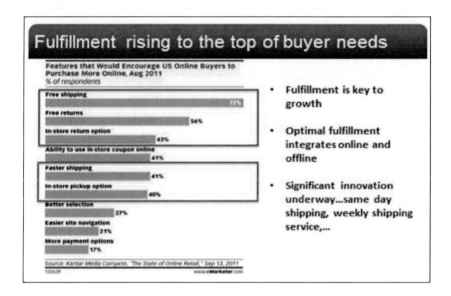

The world of retail is bigger than remote state sales taxes. When you think big picture, the higher shipping costs alone often tip the balance away from smaller retailers. There are also many direct tax benefits enjoyed by the largest retailers that never flow down to their small business competitors. These include state and local property tax breaks and sales tax exclusions. Do those who want a "level playing field" demand that all small business retailers get the same tax credits, the same sales tax exclusions and the same shipping rates? If and when they do, we will be the first to endorse changing *Quill* and lifting the prohibition against remote sales tax collection and remittance.

In short, physical presence brings real world benefits to retailers. Small retailers tend to have very limited physical presence. They enjoy the benefits of physical presence in one or two locations at most. Giant retailers have national store or distribution networks, and they enjoy the benefits over a large number of states and communities. Today, the retail benefits of physical presence come with a tax cost, and retail businesses have understood that rule for years.

The Internet sales tax bills that have been introduced in this Congress would change the playing field in a way that would apply sales taxes to small business retailers in the same manner as giant retailers. This change in law would mean that consumers would face a new tax cost on goods purchased from small remote retailers, but the consumer would not gain benefits tied to presence. This means that the shopper will be less likely to buy from small retailers on the Internet. The real world effect will be to disadvantage small business retailers, a segment of retailers that is already losing market share under the status quo. This is why these bills are anti-small business.

Current law regarding remote state sales tax authority is not perfect, and there have been problems. A few large online retailers have not operated in the spirit of the law, failing to collect sales taxes where they have physical presence. However, their smaller competitors are and do collect and remit sales taxes for purchases made both online and offline. Some states have used sales tax-related incentives to encourage local investment by said large retailers. In addition, states have not enforced their consumer Use Tax laws. These are real problems with the current system. But current remote sales tax policies for small business retailers using the Internet are a positive aspect of the current system. Protecting small business retail from blanket remote sales tax collection is beneficial for retail competition and economic growth, and should be retained in any new remote sales tax regime.

Congress has the power to address abuses and inequities without raising new costs on small business retail entrepreneurs. A real Small Business Exemption would do that. A real Small Business Exemption would protect small retailers who are already falling behind. Permanently protecting small business retailers from national remote sales tax collection burdens will promote new retail competition. Some have said that e-commerce does not need "infant industry protection." While this debate is not about an infant industry, it is about infant and small businesses. And, the reality is that there will always be small business retailers who you want to protect and allow to grow. A true Small Business Exemption will be an incubator for new businesses, who we hope will graduate into any new collection regime.

Protecting small businesses from burdens that will undermine their growth and even directly promoting small business operations is not a new or novel concept. There has traditionally been bipartisan support for small business promotion. There is an entire federal agency aimed at promoting and protecting small businesses, as you well know. Also, small businesses in the last two decades have received preferential treatment in legislation such as the Family Medical Leave Act, the Health Care Reform bills, and the Small Business Jobs Act.

If you believe that small business retailers should not be harmed by a change in remote sales tax law, then the definition of what constitutes a small business that would be preserved from new tax collection requirements is an important one. Congress traditionally delegates authority to the Small Business Administration (SBA) to set small business size standards. The SBA's unique position allows it take into account the intricate differences in diverse business models. Currently, SBA's size standard for small "electronic shopping" businesses is $30 million in total annual sales. The absolute smallest business size standard in the retail space is $7 million, used for single stand-alone newsstands and kiosks.

Every previous remote sales tax proposal until the 111th Congress has included thoughtful protections for small businesses, recognizing the playing field is unequal for small guys,. More specifically, proposals introduced in the 107th through the 110th Congresses included a small business exemption of at least $5 million, or authorized the Small Business Administration to establish the exemption threshold. And there are other widely-accepted small business definitions. As noted, the SBA defines a small retail business as a business that does between $30 million and $7 million in sales, taking into account the business model. Additionally, the Treasury Department has proposed a methodology for defining small businesses that would ultimately set the threshold at $10 million.

Unfortunately, the authors of recent remote sales tax bills have walked away from true small business protections. Starting in 2010, remote sales tax bills dropped the term "Small Business Exemption" and replaced it with the term "small seller exception". They want small businesses to be collecting online everywhere. Obviously, we disagree.

For all of these reasons, eBay strongly supports H.Res. 95. This bipartisan resolution opposes new tax collection requirements for small online businesses and entrepreneurs. The Resolution, which was introduced by your Judiciary colleagues Representatives Lungren and Lofgren, calls for policies to maintain the principle that small businesses with less presence should not be held to the same standard as large retail businesses with significant presence. eBay sincerely appreciates Congressman Lungren's and Congresswoman Lofgren's leadership on this issue. We also appreciate the 31 cosponsors that have declared their support for small business retailers by cosponsoring H.Res. 95.

To conclude, eBay's focus has been to protect small business retailers using the Internet from any new onerous tax burdens. eBay supports robust protections for small business retailers in any new remote sales tax regime, and will continue to urge members of the Committee to do the same.

I appreciate the opportunity to testify before the Committee, and I look forward to your questions.

End Notes

[1] Forrester Research: Web-Influenced Retail Sales Forecast 2010-2015 (US).
[2] ConsumerReports.org. (July 2010). *America's Top Stores: 30,000 Readers Reveal the Best Places to Shop for Practically Anything.* Consumer Reports
[3] Forrester Research: Web-Influenced Retail Sales Forecast 2010-2015 (US).
[4] Internet Retailer. http://www.internetretailer.com/top500/list/

In: Taxation of Internet Sales   ISBN: 978-1-62257-974-7
Editors: Keith Joyner and Carl Sawhill   © 2013 Nova Science Publishers, Inc.

Chapter 8

TESTIMONY OF SENATOR HOWARD KENLEY III, INDIANA SENATE. HEARING ON "CONSTITUTIONAL LIMITATIONS ON STATES' AUTHORITY TO COLLECT SALES TAXES IN E-COMMERCE"[*]

Thank you Chairman Smith, Ranking Member Conyers and Members of the Judiciary Committee for the invitation to talk to today about one of the most serious issues facing state authority over their taxes and also one of the most challenging issues in retailing.

INTRODUCTION

I am a Republican State Senator from Indiana. I chair the Senate Appropriations Committee and I am a long-time retailer. I come before you today in my role as someone responsible for producing a balanced state budget and as the president of the country's most successful business tax simplification initiative.

---

[*] This is an edited, reformatted and augmented version of the testimony given on November 30, 2011 before the House Judiciary Committee.

BACKGROUND

I appreciate the title of today's hearing: "Constitutional Limitations on State's Authority to Collect Sales Taxes on E-Commerce." When I studied the Bellas Hess case in Harvard Law School a few years after the Supreme Court's decision I never imagined I would be testifying before Congress about that Court's interpretation of the Constitution's limitations on state taxes. Unfortunately the intervening years have made this issue even more ominous for state budgets and for retailers. When the Court decided Bellas Hess this was a catalog issue and while catalogs offered greater variety than many stores, catalogs could not compete with local customer service and immediate availability. Today one day and two day delivery are normal and same day delivery is possible. On top of near immediate and almost complete hassle-free delivery local retailers must compete against near limitless variety and in many cases a 6-10% government mandated price difference.

In Quill, the US Supreme Court made it clear that a state's ability to employ an effective sales tax was going to depend on the authority granted by Congress under the Commerce Clause. I come before you today to ask you to exercise that authority.

E-COMMERCE SALES

According to the Department of Commerce e-commerce sales in 2005 were $87 billion. This year they will total more than twice that amount. The quarterly e-commerce sales in 2011 increased on average 17% more than the same quarters in 2010, while total sales increased less than 8%. While that difference may seem great, it is actually below normal for e-commerce sales. Prior to this year e-commerce sales increased at a much greater rate than did total sales. If e-commerce sales are increasing at a rate greater than total sales the difference must be sales that would have otherwise gone to a local retailer. Retailers across this country often find themselves acting at the display case for consumers who come in and try out the product but then go home and buy it on-line. The amazing power of mobile phones allows consumers to scan product codes, check prices and buy a product from another business before they even leave the first business.

COLLECTING IS TOO COMPLEX

Some will actually argue that it is impossible to collect. Every retailer today looks to automate everything that can be automated. Sales tax collection software exists, it works and it is affordable. Computer technology and supply chain management have radically changed retailing. In many ways the Internet is the perfect environment in which to collect sales taxes because sales tax collection can be automated.

IMPACT ON SMALL BUSINESS

Some opponents will argue against placing another burden on businesses and especially on small business. Unfortunately, today the burden is on those retailers who are trying to compete against someone who isn't collecting the tax. That 6-10% government mandated price advantage is the real burden on small business. However, all of the bills introduced in this Congress protect small businesses by excluding the smallest, by requiring states to simplify their laws and processes, and by requiring states to provide software.

COLLECTING IS A TAX INCREASE

Some opponents will tell you these bills are a tax increase. It is not true that paying a tax you owe, but were not paying, is a tax increase. If this theory were taken to its logical extreme every audit assessment would be a tax increase since someone is being forced to pay a tax they hadn't paid. The obligation to pay exists today. Asking one retailer to collect without asking the same of all retailers doesn't seem like equal protection under the law.

STATES HAVE NOT DONE ENOUGH TO COLLECT THE TAX OWED TODAY

Some opponents will say the states don't do a good enough job collecting the use tax. There are only two ways to collect this tax: have the retailer collect it or educate and then audit consumers. There is nothing more inefficient than conducting an audit and I disagree with those who argue that states should engage in more audits.

STATES HAVE NOT SIMPLIFIED ENOUGH

Some opponents will say the states have not simplified their tax systems enough to warrant Congressional authority. In 1967 the Supreme Court said that with the various sales tax systems and the very limited technology that then existed was too much to allow states to require everyone to collect. What the Supreme Court didn't answer was how much simpler the sales tax system would have to be and what technology would have to exist to rule differently. Technology has changed in every possible way since 1967. The debate since the Supreme Court's decision is how much simplification must be done, and that is a decision best left to Congress to decide.

In: Taxation of Internet Sales   ISBN: 978-1-62257-974-7
Editors: Keith Joyner and Carl Sawhill   © 2013 Nova Science Publishers, Inc.

Chapter 9

TESTIMONY OF PAUL MISENER, VICE PRESIDENT FOR GLOBAL PUBLIC POLICY, AMAZON.COM. HEARING ON "CONSTITUTIONAL LIMITATIONS ON STATES' AUTHORITY TO COLLECT SALES TAXES IN E-COMMERCE"[*]

Thank you, Chairman Smith and Ranking Member Conyers, for inviting me to testify. Amazon has long supported an even-handed federal framework for state sales tax collection and, to that end, we have participated in the Streamlined Sales Tax Project for over a decade, and we are pleased to participate in this hearing. Amazon strongly supports enactment of a federal bill with appropriate provisions.

Mr. Chairman, Congress – and only Congress – may, should, and feasibly can authorize the states to require out-of-state sellers to collect the sales tax already owed.

At the Philadelphia Convention, which the Founders convened principally to consider the challenging issue of trade among the states, Congress was granted exclusive power to regulate interstate commerce. Exactly two centuries later, in 1987, North Dakota challenged this exclusivity and, following five years of litigation, the U.S. Supreme Court held in *Quill v. North Dakota* that requiring out-of-state sellers to collect tax would impose an unconstitutional burden on interstate commerce. The *Quill* court also

---

[*] This is an edited, reformatted and augmented version of the testimony given on November 30, 2011 before the House Judiciary Committee.

confirmed that Congress eventually could "disagree with our conclusions" and that this issue is "not Testimony of Paul Misener only one that Congress may be better qualified to resolve, but also one that Congress has the ultimate power to resolve."

Far from an e-commerce "loophole," the constitutional limitation on states' authority to collect sales tax is at the core of our Nation's founding principles. For this reason, Amazon has steadfastly opposed state attempts to require out-of-state sellers to collect absent congressional authorization.

Mr. Chairman, Congress *should* authorize the states to require collection, with the great objects of protecting states' rights, addressing the states' needs, and leveling the playing field for all sellers.

States' rights should be protected. States need the freedom to make their own revenue policy choices. For example, Texas has chosen to eschew personal income tax, and that decision makes the Texas budget particularly sensitive to uncollected sales tax. The right of Texas to make this policy choice effective should be protected. Congress should protect the states' rights, and authorize them to require collection of sales tax revenue already owed, and doing so would not violate pledges that are limited to questions of income tax rates and deductions.

The states' financial needs should be addressed. The states face serious budget shortfalls, yet the federal government faces its own fiscal challenges. Congress should help address the states' budget shortfalls without spending federal funds, by authorizing the states to require collection of the billions of revenue dollars already owed.

Fairness among sellers should be created and maintained. Sellers should compete on a level playing field. Congress should not exempt too many sellers from collection, for these sellers will obtain a lasting *un*-level playing field versus Main Street and other retailers. Congress should rectify the current imbalance and avoid a future imbalance.

Mr. Chairman, Congress feasibly *can* authorize the states to require collection. The facts in the *Quill* decision arose a quarter of a century ago, and the Supreme Court's decision was rendered a year before the World Wide Web was invented. With today's computing and communications technology, widespread collection no longer would be an unconstitutional burden on interstate commerce, and Congress feasibly can authorize the states to require all but the very smallest volume sellers to collect.

Much attention has been paid to the size of a "small seller exception" threshold in federal legislation – and rightfully so. Such a threshold, which would exempt some sellers from a collection requirement, must be kept very low to attain the objectives of protecting states' rights, addressing the states' needs, and creating fairness among sellers.

In this context, several kinds of small volume sellers must be considered.

Foremost are the Main Street small business retailers who, unless the small seller exception threshold is kept very low, will forever face an un-level playing field compared to a newly-created exempt class of out-of-state sellers.

Next are the online advertising affiliates, tens of thousands of whom have lost jobs or income as the result of ineffective, counterproductive sales tax laws recently enacted in a half-dozen states. Congress should act to make such laws uninteresting and irrelevant to the states – and thereby immediately restore the lost jobs and income – by authorizing the states to require collection.

Small volume online sellers have received most of the attention, and not without reason. No one wants these sellers to shoulder alone burdens compared to those faced by the small business retailers who already collect sales tax in our local communities. Yet no one should want these online sellers to take advantage of a newly-created *un*-level playing field over small Main Street businesses, and no one should want government to pick business model winners and losers this way.

The consequences of the threshold level to states' rights, the states' needs, and fairness are very significant, because a surprisingly large fraction of e-commerce is conducted by smaller volume sellers. For example, nearly 30% of uncollected sales tax revenue today is attributable to sellers with annual online sales below $150,000, and only one percent of online sellers sell more than this amount. In other words, a $150,000 exception would deny the states nearly 30% of the newly-available (yet already owed) revenue, but would exempt from collection 99% of online sellers. Any higher threshold would deny the states even more revenue and keep the playing field even more un-level.

Fortunately, today's computing and communications technology will allow all online sellers to collect and remit tax like Main Street retailers.

Large volume online sellers already have and use this technology. Amazon and Overstock, for example, collect tax on sales to consumers in states where our retail businesses have nexus. And the online arms of large multichannel retailers collect in the states where they have retail stores. Quite obviously, state sales tax can be collected nationwide, at least by larger volume sellers like Amazon, Overstock, and the multichannel stores, for they have the technology.

This technology is not limited to large sellers. Rather, service providers also make the technology available to medium and small volume sellers. Thus, collection is either *by* sellers or *for* sellers. There are many service providers already: ADP, Avalara, and FedTax, for example.

Two other examples come to mind: Amazon and eBay.

Both companies use sophisticated computing and communications technology to serve their seller customers. But, while Amazon is prepared to make its technology available as a service to help sellers by collecting sales tax for them, eBay seeks to avoid any role in collection, claiming that small volume sellers will be burdened and, implicitly, that eBay's technology is not capable of helping its largest sellers to collect. And these claims are made despite the fact that eBay manages to collect the transaction fees it charges its sellers, and despite the fact that eBay already calculates state sales tax for eBay sellers, all the way down to the local jurisdiction level. Amazon and many other service providers will help smaller online sellers collect; surely eBay can as well.

In conclusion, Mr. Chairman, Congress may, should, and feasibly can attain the objectives of protecting states' rights, addressing the states' needs without federal spending, and leveling the playing field for all sellers – but only if any "small seller exception" is kept very low.

The time to act is nigh. Amazon is grateful for this hearing, and we look forward to working with you and your colleagues in Congress to pass appropriate legislation as soon as possible.

Thank you. I look forward to your questions.

In: Taxation of Internet Sales   ISBN: 978-1-62257-974-7
Editors: Keith Joyner and Carl Sawhill   © 2013 Nova Science Publishers, Inc.

Chapter 10

STATEMENT OF CONGRESSWOMAN JACKIE SPEIER. HEARING ON THE "MARKETPLACE EQUITY ACT OF 2011"[*]

Chairman Smith, Ranking Member Conyers and members, thank you for allowing me to be here today to discuss this important issue and HR 3179—the Marketplace Equity Act. I am very proud to have partnered with Congressman Womack on this truly bi-partisan effort. If a Republican from Arkansas and a Democrat from California can come together on a bill that deals with tax issues, then the time really has come to finally resolve this issue. And this is an issue that ONLY Congress can resolve.

The fundamental unfairness in the marketplace and in our communities that this bill addresses has grown dramatically over the past few years. When Quill was decided by the Supreme Court in 1992, the internet and the World Wide Web did not even exist as a retail marketplace. Sales taxes were collected on almost all retail sales. But according to the Commerce department, online retail sales have increased 300% to $224 Billion over the past eight years, and they are expected to almost triple again over the next eight to more than $600 billion—overtaking sales at brick and mortar stores. This is clearly not a business model in its infancy.

And there should be no doubt that this is not a new tax. Consumers owe sales and use tax for these purchases in all states with a sales tax, but only about one percent actually pays them. This is an issue of collection and fairness. Some retailers have to collect the tax from the consumer, and some don't, for the very same product.

---

[*] This is an edited, reformatted and augmented version of the testimony given on July 24, 2012 before the House Judiciary Committee.

State and local governments impose sales taxes to help pay for essential public services such as police, firefighters, and teachers. As online sales grow, the financial hit to our communities gets more severe. Each sales tax dollar not collected is a service not provided and a possible job lost—these are cuts to police, fire departments and schools. I have seen it happen in my district, and I am sure it is happening in all of your districts. Almost $7 out of every $10 spent at a local brick and mortar retailer stays local. More than $4 out of every $10 spent at a national retailer stays local. But none of the money spent at an online-only retailer stays in the community. The only option left to state and local governments facing even greater loses as more retail shifts to the internet will be to raise taxes.

We have all seen it--large online-only retailers have been able to trample the small retailers in all of our communities through the big price advantage of not charging sales tax. Across the United States, the brick and mortar stores who can compete on price but can't compete with tax-free online sales are closing, and jobs are being lost. Brick and mortar retailers create four jobs for every one job created by an online retailer.

In a state like California, that sales tax price advantage is huge, particularly at a time when financially strapped consumers are looking for ways to stretch their dollars as far as possible. Technology has now made it possible for them to shop for goods in brick and mortar stores, get advice and kick the tires on products like TVs and computers and cameras and bicycles, and then find and buy the item online—sometimes right on their mobile phone while still standing in the store.

Eric McCrystal, who runs a small powertools company in my district in San Carlos, told me it happens regularly—people come in and test his power tools and then go online to buy because they can escape the sales tax--even though it is owed. This simply isn't fair to the merchants like Eric who have invested in a storefront and hired employees to provide a service. And ultimately it isn't fair to the taxpayer who has a legal obligation to pay but isn't able to easily fulfill it or doesn't even know they owe the tax, and could be subject to audit and penalties for failure to pay.

But there are also lots of people turning to the online marketplace to expand their small businesses or to reinvent themselves after losing their job. Those legitimately small online businesses are exempted from having to collect sales taxes under this bill —but *only* until they too become sophisticated marketplace actors.

The same way technology has made it easy for online shopping, technology has made it much simpler for online retailers to collect sales taxes.

And since Congress must grant this authority to the states, our bill provides a very simple framework for states to opt in to this framework. It also requires states to provide the tools and services required to comply *cost-free* to online retailers. This is certainly more than brick and mortar retailers get.

Once upon a time there was a valid argument that the internet marketplace was in its infancy and we didn't want to stifle its development. Those days are gone. Companies like Amazon and Overstock.com are proof of it. California is expected to lose more than $1.8 billion in uncollected tax revenue this year alone, and the amount is going up every year as more purchases are made through online retailers that have become expert at gaming the system to avoid the obligation to collect and remit sales taxes.

The failure of Congress to address this issue has led to more, not less confusion in the marketplace. Instead of a national approach, desperate states are taking their own actions in response to this problem—there are the Streamline states, the Amazon deals, and the states that have expanded the reach of nexus through legislatiion. At least 30 states have taken some action to try and increase their sales tax collections on online sales.

Rather than hide its head in the sand, Congress could solve this issue for all states by allowing states to require online sellers to collect tax even if they do not meet a physical presence test. It could set the conditions that states must satisfy if they wish to do so, ensuring that it is simple and not unduly burdensome, while at the same time respecting states' rights. That is precisely what the Marketplace Equity Act does.

In: Taxation of Internet Sales ISBN: 978-1-62257-974-7
Editors: Keith Joyner and Carl Sawhill © 2013 Nova Science Publishers, Inc.

Chapter 11

STATEMENT OF HANNS KUTTNER, VISITING FELLOW, HUDSON INSTITUTE. HEARING ON THE "MARKETPLACE EQUITY ACT OF 2011"[*]

I'm Hanns Kuttner, a Visiting Fellow at Hudson Institute. From Hudson's founding in 1961, it has been an organization of people with an interest in the nature of the future. I appreciate this opportunity to offer a perspective on the future of buying and selling.

Within the past year we provided a view of the future of buying and selling with a focus on issues that relate to today's hearing: how advances in technology will change the role of place in where buyers and sellers are located. We gave this report the title, "Future Marketplace: Free and Fair" because that title reflects how technology and the sales tax are one force giving shape to the future of the marketplace.

Before turning to some of the details of the report, let me start with a discussion of innovation, something that might be seen as a digression, but to me is essential to understanding the issues you are sorting through.

Innovation is the source of improvement in our standard of living. We live different lives than those who came before us because of innovations in technology and how technology gets put to use.

In the late 1960's, Herman Kahn, who founded the Hudson Institute, along with Hudson colleagues, published a look at the future entitled, "The Year 2000: A Framework for Speculation on the Next Thirty Three Years." Now

---

[*] This is an edited, reformatted and augmented version of the testimony given on July 24, 2012 before the House Judiciary Committee.

that it is past the year 2000, we have the ability to look back and see what they got right and what didn't turn out as they expected. They made it easy to assess their work by including a list of 100 innovations they thought possible.

Looking over the list, the ones that were most likely to be realized were those that had to do with communications and information technology. "Personalized pagers" have both come about and been surpassed. Similarly with "home computers." Those that have not turned out as expected are in such categories as energy and transportation.

One thing I see in looking at the list of innovations realized and not is how important changes in relative prices are for innovations that have come about and those that have not.

The whole world of information technology and its role in our economy is overshadowed by Moore's Law. When first propounded in the 1960's, it expressed a relationship between the number of transistors on integrated circuits and the time it takes to develop a circuit with twice as many transistors. For our purposes, what is important is the impact on prices. When you can double capacity without increasing price, there is a strong effect on relative prices. Whatever gets made cheaper, you'll buy more of; what's been made relatively more expensive, you'll buy less.

The areas where the possibilities seen in the late 1960s have been realized have been those where the changes in relative prices have been the greatest. We got the "personal pagers," and a lot more. We didn't get the innovations in sources of energy because changes in relative prices have not occurred. Had improvements in solar collectors occurred at the same pace as integrated circuits, we would have been more likely to be a world in which solar power dominated electricity generation.

Developments in technology determine what is possible; changes in relative prices determine how extensively those technologies get used.

Today I can use a search engine to find more references in a second than I could in a whole year in a library a generation ago. I used Google to search for "relative prices" and got 714,000 results in .45 seconds. And the cost to me was free. Lewis Strauss, who chaired the Atomic Energy Commission in the 1950s, got it right with his formulation that the children of that generation would experience a world with something that would be "too cheap to meter," except it would turn out to be information, not electricity.

It is change in relative prices which is behind the degree to which we adopt new technologies. Many generations of integrated circuits ago, a smart phone would have cost $2,500 rather than a tenth or less of that price. At that price, many fewer people would have adopted this technology.

Were my Hudson colleagues and I to revisit Herman Kahn's 1967 project and offer our musings about the world 33 years hence, many of the possibilities would no doubt embody an element of information technology. While one reason to do that would be seeing the potential for new technologies, the more important reason would be changes in relative prices. Technology that involves information will be both quicker and faster, but more importantly, cheaper.

Concepts that require vast amounts of information are at the core of many of the most interesting innovations of our time. The challenge for thinking about what might be possible in the future is thinking through how those vast amounts can be put together in a way that users find simple and attractive.

This brings me back to the topic of your hearing today.

Like all other sectors, the buying and selling of services has felt the impact of the change in relative prices of information. The early innovations reflected the technological possibilities of the times. Benjamin Franklin is said to have been America's first catalog seller. Catalogs made it possible to sell things to people without buyer and seller meeting up, either via a buyer coming into a store or a seller, such as the country peddler, knocking on the buyer's door.

It's easier to adapt existing categories to explain a new innovation. The use of the Internet to bring buyers and sellers together through that medium could initially have been described as "electronic catalogs," buy anyone who has bought something via a catalog and looked at what is possible through the Internet now would find "electronic catalog" an inadequate way to describe what is possible through the Internet.

We have the same challenge in thinking about what is yet to come. Information technology is making physical location less important across many domains. Buying and selling is one of those. In our report, we offered some possibilities. Beyond those, there are possibilities whose shape is yet difficult to discern that involve the implications of "big data" and monitors and sensors. While all is in the range of speculation, an example could involve methods that learn how fast we use up household commodities and automatically order more. Running out of toilet paper would then be a thing of the past. These kinds of purchases would be made possible by information technology, but in ways very different from the idea of someone going to a web site and following a process to make a purchase.

This notion of changes in relative prices and how information in particular has a relatively lower price is central to the issues you are grappling with today.

Differences in relative prices can be seen in the structure of the sales tax that states adopted in the 1930s. In the throes of the Depression, state governments began to introduce a general sales tax.

While the tax is a tax on those who purchase goods and services, the structure of the tax reflects the fact that the sellers have much larger scale and hence could collect and remit the sales tax much more efficiently. While I owe tax, the seller collects it and sends it to the state.

One could imagine a sales tax collected in a much different way. This alternative sales tax would be collected via returns completed by buyers. This alternative would be much more administratively burdensome than the sales tax we actually have. Buyers would be responsible for keeping receipts and periodically totaling up receipts and remitting the tax owed. The yield from the same tax rate would be much lower as individuals didn't remember all their purchases; to produce the same amount of revenue would require a higher tax rate. Enforcing the tax might involve individual audits that would be intrusive and not produce much revenue per return audited.

Comparing this version of the sales tax to the version we have, we can see how much more efficient it is to have sellers keep track of sales and remit the sales tax amount on behalf of purchasers. The society-wide burden of administering the current tax is much lower than the alternative way of administering the sales tax I've described.

For reasons relating to the history of the Supreme Court's interpretation of the Commerce Clause, the presence or absence of a state line between the location of the buyer and seller has become important for the administration of the sales tax.

States felt they could not use the same approach for collecting the sales tax when buyer and seller were in different states. Rather than favor out-of-state sellers, they adopted a use tax which follows the less-efficient "buyer collects" approach.

The weaknesses of the use tax include the higher burden on the taxpayer per unit of revenue collected and the spotty pattern of tax collection. Corporations which have tax departments staffed with skilled professionals carefully monitor tax obligation and pay taxes owed. Individuals are not much bothered to pay the tax nor do they appear to invest much effort in trying to comply.

As we noted in our report on the future of the marketplace for goods and services, in a market that is both free and fair, everybody plays by the same rules. The effect of the history of the Commerce Clause has been to create two sets of rules, one for sales where the sellers are in the same state and another where they are in different states.

The distortion that results from having two sets of rules is the difference in prices between the two sets of rules. In one, the buyer acts based on a price that includes the sales tax. In the other, the buyer may not see the sales tax.

This year, we estimate that this distortion will impact $330 billion worth of sales. In future years, that amount would likely be higher because of the continued change in relative prices. Innovation, in information technology and logistics, will expand the potential of what can be bought and sold through the Internet and other communications technologies. However, one pattern that has become clearer since we completed our report is that more sellers are losing their "out of state" status and becoming responsible for collecting the sales tax in more and more states.

As the Supreme Court framed the issue, the Commerce Clause raises the question of what is an "undue burden" on out-of-state sellers. The ongoing decline in the cost of information is reducing the cost of compliance.

The year in which the Supreme Court last considered this empirical question was 1992. At that time, the Internet was just emerging from the research community, search engines had not yet been invented, and a cell phone had the size that approached that of a loaf of bread.

Among the pieces of information whose price has declined since that time is the cost of learning what the sales tax is in any particular jurisdiction or in what jurisdiction a particular Zip Plus Four mailing address is located. "Google it," is a common phrase of our era. While a piece of information may be embedded in a complex table, our ability to get at it through search engines has made the complex seem simple.

Ensuring that the future marketplace is both free and fair requires taking into account the ongoing decline in the relative price of this information.

In: Taxation of Internet Sales   ISBN: 978-1-62257-974-7
Editors: Keith Joyner and Carl Sawhill   © 2013 Nova Science Publishers, Inc.

Chapter 12

STATEMENT OF STEVE DELBIANCO, EXECUTIVE DIRECTOR, NETCHOICE. HEARING ON THE "MARKETPLACE EQUITY ACT OF 2011"*

Chairman Smith, Ranking Member Conyers, and members of the committee: thank you for holding this hearing on HR 3179 and the "internet tax" debate. My name is Steve DelBianco, and I serve as Executive Director of NetChoice, a coalition of leading e-commerce and online companies promoting the value, convenience, and choice of Internet business models. NetChoice members include industry leaders such as eBay, Expedia, Facebook, LivingSocial, NewsCorp, Overstock, VeriSign, and Yahoo, plus several thousand small businesses that go online to reach their customers.

NetChoice has been deeply engaged on Internet tax issues for over a decade, including recent media debates in the Wall Street Journal and on CNBC, Marketplace radio, CNN, and PBS. Since 2004, we have participated in meetings of the Streamlined Sales Tax Project (SSTP), a long-term effort that HR 3179 seeks to sweep aside.

NetChoice is a founding member of TruST, the coalition for True Simplification of Taxation, a new group whose association members also include: the American Catalog Mailers Association; the Direct Marketing Association; and the Electronic Retailing Association. (www.True Simplification.org) Each coalition member has submitted written statements

---

* This is an edited, reformatted and augmented version of the testimony given on July 24, 2012 before the House Judiciary Committee.

for today's hearing, and we respectfully ask that their statements be included as part of the hearing record.

In this testimony we are discussing legislation that would authorize states to impose sales tax obligations on out-of-state businesses (HR 3179). Our major points are:

1. For businesses without stores or distribution centers in multiple states, HR 3179 would allow states to *impose a new tax* with uniquely complex burdens of nearly 10,000 tax jurisdictions in 46 states.
2. HR 3179 *does not require nearly enough sales tax simplification* to justify imposing significant new burdens on out-of-state businesses.
3. The new tax burdens imposed by HR 3179 are *not justified by anticipated revenue*, since total potential sales tax on all consumer e-commerce is well below one percent of total state & local tax revenue.
4. HR 3179 *does not adequately protect America's small businesses*, for whom new collection burdens would be disproportionately complex and expensive.

The House Judiciary committee is ideally positioned to deliberate whether to expand state taxing powers to include out-of-state businesses and citizens. To help with that deliberation, we begin with some straight answers to critical questions.

WHY DON'T ONLINE RETAILERS PAY SALES TAX TO EVERY STATE?

Last November, the editors of the Wall Street Journal asked NetChoice whether all online retailers should have to pay sales tax to every state. My argument in the published debate began with this:

Should online retailers have to collect sales tax? Yes, and they already do.

Just like all retailers, online stores must collect sales tax for every state where they have a physical presence. That's why Amazon.com adds sales tax to orders from customers in the 5 states where it has facilities. But Amazon and online retailers aren't required to collect tax for other states, leaving those customers to pay a "use tax" that states rarely enforce against individual taxpayers. This framework frustrates state tax collectors and businesses that compete with online retailers. But when we learn how this physical presence requirement evolved, it becomes clear why we should retain this standard for imposing new tax collection burdens on online retailers.[1]

As members of this committee know, today's physical presence standard is based on Article 1 of the US Constitution, designed 225 years ago to stop states from impeding interstate commerce. The Commerce Clause was a necessary condition to unite the independent colonies, since they had a legacy of imposing customs duties and trade barriers to favor in-state businesses.

Fast-forward to the 1960s, when state tax collectors wanted catalog retailers to collect their sales taxes, even where those catalogs had no operations in the state. The US Supreme Court relied on the Commerce Clause in deciding that states could not impose tax collection requirements on catalogs "whose only connection with customers in the State is by common carrier or the United States mail."[2]

In 1992, the Supreme Court took another look at tax collection by an office products catalog company by the name of Quill.[3] Seeing a patchwork of rates and rules for several thousand sales tax jurisdictions, the Court again held that requiring out-of-state companies to collect and remit taxes was so complicated that it presented an unreasonable burden on interstate commerce.

Moreover, the Supreme Court was not moved by the state's argument that computer technology created the necessary simplification. Instead, the Supreme Court acknowledged the lower court's finding that advances in computer technology had eased the burdens of tax collection, but still found the requirement of tax collection unduly burdensome.[4]

Quill was not concerned with "fairness." While some argued fairness as justification for tax collection, "[i]n contrast, the Commerce Clause and its nexus requirement are informed ***not so much by concerns about fairness*** for the individual [state] as by ***structural concerns about the effects of state regulation on the national economy***."[5]

Quill is the law of the land today, protecting businesses from sales tax imposition by states where that business has no physical presence, while requiring businesses to pay sales tax for every state where they do have a physical presence.

WOULD HR 3179 CREATE A NEW TAX?

State sales tax laws put obligations on both buyers and sellers in order to maximize tax revenue collection. States levy a sales tax on sellers within their jurisdiction, and it's up to the seller whether to pass that tax along to buyers. Most sellers do pass the tax along to buyers, whether at the cash register, online, or over the phone. But after an audit, a seller is liable for any sales tax they were obliged to collect but failed to do so, even when the seller can't recover the tax from those previous customers.

For example, Michigan "sales tax" is actually a tax on the privilege of doing business in the state:

> ... there shall be collected from all persons engaged in the business of making sales at retail, by which ownership of tangible personal property is transferred for consideration, **an annual tax for the privilege of engaging in that business** equal to 6% of the gross proceeds of the business, plus the penalty and interest if applicable ...[6]

As in all state sales tax statutes, the Michigan sales tax is the personal liability of the seller. The seller is allowed, but not obligated, to pass the tax along to the consumer. Today, only businesses that have presence in Michigan are required to pay a tax for the privilege of engaging in business there. HR 3179 would enable Michigan to impose its "privilege" tax on businesses with no facilities, no vote, and no voice in Michigan. The fact that the tax can be passed on to Michigan consumers does not make it any less a *new tax burden* for businesses all over the country.

Arizona and California use the same approach, imposing their sales tax for the "privilege" of selling goods to state residents, even if shipped via common carriers:

> "The Arizona transaction privilege tax is commonly referred to as a sales tax; however, the tax is on the privilege of doing business in Arizona and is not a true sales tax. Although the transaction privilege tax is usually passed on to the consumer, it is actually a tax on the vendor."[7]
>
> California: "The sales tax portion of any sales and use tax ordinance adopted under this part shall be imposed for the privilege of selling tangible personal property at retail"[8]

Clearly, sales tax is due from *sellers* whose activities or locations create enough of a physical presence for a state to impose collection obligations. But if Congress overturns the *Quill* standard, businesses would be forced to pay a new tax to states where they have no physical presence. Most of those businesses would pass the tax along to their customers, but make no mistake about it – the states will demand that businesses pay the new tax — whether or not their customers were charged.

HAVEN'T STATES SIMPLIFIED THEIR SALES TAX SYSTEMS? WHAT ABOUT THE SSTP INITIATIVE?

The Supreme Court's *Quill* decision also made it clear that states could simplify their sales tax systems and come back to the Supreme Court and show that they have truly eliminated the unreasonable burden on interstate commerce.

But instead, a handful of states chose to skip the harsh judgment of the Court and go directly to Congress to request the power to impose these burdens on out-of-state businesses. Their efforts began a decade ago with the Streamlined Sales Tax Project (SSTP).

Despite a decade of concerted effort, the actual simplifications achieved by the SSTP are not nearly sufficient to justify Congress abandoning its role in protecting interstate commerce. Rather, the SSTP has shown that *simplification has become just a slogan – not a standard.*

First, critics cite the fact that SSTP originally promised just one tax rate per state, but now accommodates over 9,600 local jurisdictions,[9] each with its own tax rates and sales tax holidays. That's up from 7,800 jurisdictions in the 20 years since *Quill*, and still growing. This makes the US a true outlier when it comes to sales tax jurisdictions. The European Union has 27 jurisdictions for Value Added Tax (VAT) and India lets each state have a single tax rate, but we are the only country where sales tax is controlled at the local government level.

Second, the SSTP has abandoned many of its original simplification requirements. For example, the SSTP no longer contains required compensation for all retailers and has all but eliminated the small seller exception. In an effort to attract states with origin sourcing, the SSTP abandoned one sourcing rule and now allows both origin and destination-based regimes. To entice Massachusetts to join SSTP, the Governing Board voted to allow thresholds for certain clothing items, even though thresholds were one of the most complex elements it pledged to simplify. (Notwithstanding this allowance, Massachusetts has not jet joined SSTP.)

Despite these concessions, less than half of eligible states have joined SSTP (only 22 full member states in SSTP, out of 46 states that have sales tax).

WHY IS SSTP LOSING MOMENTUM WHEN STATES EXPECT TO RECEIVE BILLIONS OF DOLLARS IN NEW TAX REVENUE?

Some argue that SSTP is losing momentum because non-member states are reluctant to let unelected tax administrators make decisions about tax rules and determine compliance. More likely however, SSTP is losing momentum because states began to see the revenue estimates as wildly inflated.

A simple calculation using government data shows that the maximum sales tax potential for consumer e-commerce *is less than one percent of total state and local tax revenue*:

> Start with the US Department of Commerce's *2010 Electronic Commerce Industry Assessment,* which reported total retail e-commerce of $169 billion.[10]
> Apply an average tax rate of 7 percent, giving total potential sales tax of $11.8 billion.
> Divide that by total state and local tax revenue in 2010, reported as $1.3 trillion by the Commerce Department.[11]

The result is clear: the maximum potential sales tax on all e-commerce is less than one percent of state & local tax revenue - *assuming that no sales taxes are collected by e-retailers.*

But under *Quill*, e-retailers already collect sales tax for states where they have physical presence, as seen in the table at right. NetChoice commissioned a study by economists Robert Litan and Jeffrey Eisenach to determine where e-retailers were already collecting sales tax for web sales.

They concluded that uncollected sales tax on e-commerce in 2010 was $4.2 billion nationwide, or *less than one-third of one percent of total state and local tax revenue.*[12] This relatively small incremental revenue does not justify a dramatic expansion of state taxing powers and new collection burdens on remote businesses.

Company	States
Amazon.com	5
Staples	44
Dell	46
Office Depot	46
Apple	46
OfficeMax	46
Sears	46
CDW	46
Newegg	3
Best Buy	46
QVC	46
SonyStyle.com	46
Walmart.com	46
Costco Wholesale	38
J.C. Penney	46
HP Office	46
Circuit City Stores	29
Victoria's Secret	45
Target	46
Systemax	5

ISN'T THERE INCREASED MOMENTUM TO OVERTURN QUILL?

Recently, despite flagging momentum and diminishing revenue estimates, members of this committee have surely noticed increased lobbying efforts to overturn *Quill's* physical presence test and authorize states to collect from remote retailers. Aside from the usual tax proponents in state government, the renewed push is coming from big-box retailers.

Big-box retail chains are pushing hard for federal legislation for a simple and predictable reason: it serves *their* interests. Even a little simplification helps a big-box retailer who must already collect tax for most states, as seen in this list. Big-box retailers now have expansive web-stores of their own and give customers the convenience of doing pickups and returns at their local stores. These chains use plenty of local public services wherever they have stores, so they must collect sales tax in all their states – as required under current law. The Eisenach study looked at sales collection practices for the top 500 e-retailers, and found that 17 of the top 20 already collect in at least 38 of the 46 sales tax states.

Another way that overturning *Quill* would also help big-box retailers is that it would force tax collection costs on their biggest online competitor, Amazon.

WHY WOULD AMAZON.COM SUPPORT OVERTURNING QUILL?

Big--box retailers have aggressively gone after Amazon in the states, lobbying for new "Amazon Tax" laws declaring that Amazon already has physical presence by virtue of its advertising affiliates, distribution centers, or other subsidiaries in the state. The big-box retailers also lobbied for a new tax reporting law in Colorado, which was enjoined by a federal court as a violation of the Commerce Clause.[13] Despite the setback in Colorado and pending court challenges of the "Amazon Tax" in New York and Illinois, this aggressive and expensive state lobbying campaign has succeeded in creating well-publicized tax compliance problems for Amazon. Those problems have helped to drive Amazon to support federal legislation to overturn *Quill*.

But there's another reason for Amazon's about-face: the company is changing its business model by adding distribution centers in new states to enable faster delivery to customers. Amazon is also adding drop-boxes in convenience stores and marketing daily deals to local merchants. As a result, Amazon will have physical presence in 14 states by 2014[14] – requiring Amazon to *collect sales tax for more than half of all Americans*. And as Amazon opens more distribution centers across the country they will continue to increase their tax collection requirements.

Like the big-box stores, Amazon would reduce its tax compliance costs if states adopted even tiny steps toward simplification. Moreover, Amazon and big--box chains benefit if Congress allows states to impose new tax collection burdens on their smaller online-only competitors.

To impose expensive collection burdens on small sellers would be grossly unfair, which brings us to the aspect of "fairness" in the debate over new Internet sales taxes.

Is This Debate Really about "Fairness"?

The Constitution's Commerce clause is not about ensuring fairness. As explained above, it was all about preventing unreasonable barriers to interstate commerce, such as the customs duties imposed by the independent states before they united. In fact, *Quill* explicitly dismissed the fairness argument, saying the "Commerce Clause and its nexus requirement are informed not so much by concerns about fairness" but rather "the effects of state regulation on the national economy."[15]

"Fairness" is what you get *when everyone plays by the same rules*. And today, with *Quill* in place, all online and offline businesses play by exactly the same rule: all retailers collect sales tax for every state where they choose to have a physical presence.

Ironically, in many states the fairness argument cuts the other way. A retail store on main street collects sales tax for just the one jurisdiction where it's located. But an online retailer operating right upstairs must collect and remit for each of the local towns and counties whenever it ships within the state. In some states that means collecting for several hundred local tax jurisdictions, each with its own rates and rules. Yet when customers from surrounding towns walk in the door, the store collects and files only in the local jurisdiction.

Again, all retailers collect sales tax for every state where they choose to have a physical presence. I say, "choose" because it is the business that chooses whether to be just an online retailer or to operate physically in multiple states. When a business chooses to open stores or put sales reps in another state, it accepts the obligation to collect that state's sales tax.

And *there's actually little evidence that retailers who do collect sales tax are losing significant sales to catalog and online retailers who collect sales tax only for their home state customers.*

That makes sense, since sales tax and shipping costs aren't added until a consumer's online shopping cart goes to checkout. So comparison shoppers are usually comparing prices *before* adding any tax and shipping charges. Moreover, online shoppers usually pay shipping and handling charges that offset any tax that's not collected on most commodities. Most shoppers go online for the convenience and selection availability, not to avoid taxes. And while small and expensive electronics are a notable exception, tax proponents have shown no data indicating that significant numbers of electronics shoppers deliberately choose out--of--state online retailers just so they can avoid paying sales tax.

The argument that remote sellers have an unfair advantage just doesn't hold up. Paying sales tax for thousands of jurisdictions in 46 states is far more expensive and complex than paying sales tax for a single jurisdiction on over-the-counter purchases. Moreover, state and local governments often provide incentives and benefits to in-state retailers, such as tax increment financing, transportation improvements, worker training subsidies, grants, tax credits, etc. None of these benefits are available to out-of-state businesses.

E-COMMERCE IS THE BEST HOPE FOR MAIN STREET TO COMPETE WITH BIG-BOX STORES

Those who make the fairness claim about online versus offline are missing the far greater fairness concern of smaller retailers competing against big-box chain stores.

For decades, "main street" retailers have been getting battered by Walmart and other national chains. To survive, many main street retailers have gone online with their own web stores or with e-commerce platforms to serve repeat customers and to find new customers across the country. For example, the specialty retailer SilverGallery.com has a warehouse and store—located on Main Street—in Waynesboro, Virginia. SilverGallery, which was featured in a Wall Street Journal article last year, does some walk-in trade, but most sales come from their web store and other online channels.[16] Online sales growth enabled SilverGallery to buy their building and increase employment, right there on Main Street.

The last decade has seen another body blow delivered by big-box chains, who integrated their website operation with their stores in every city and town. Customers love the savings of doing in-store pickups to avoid shipping charges. And they love the convenience of returning online purchases to stores for exchange or credit – instead of packaging returns and standing in line at the post office. But small sellers like SilverGallery can't afford to open stores in every state. It's yet another advantage that big retailers have over small businesses with websites. The big chains also negotiate much lower rates for advertising, shipping costs, and health insurance, too.

Next comes the knockout punch for small retailers. Overturning *Quill* may be good news for big-box retailers with websites, since they already have to collect in nearly all states. But overturning *Quill* will definitely raise costs and prices for small businesses that compete – and survive – via their web and catalog sales.

WHAT IS THE IMPACT ON SMALL BUSINESSES IF THEY ARE REQUIRED TO PAY SALES TAX TO 46 STATES?

What costs would a small business face if Congress forced them to pay sales tax to all 46 states? The SST's own Cost of Collection[17] study found that a small business (under $1M in annual sales) spends 17 cents for every tax dollar it collects for states. And even if tax software works as promised, that only helps with 2 cents of the 17 cents in costs per dollar collected. *That leaves small businesses with a 15% cost burden on every dollar they collect,* for things such as:

- Paying computer consultants to integrate new tax software into their home-grown or customized systems for point-of-sale, web shopping cart, fulfillment, and accounting
- Training customer support and back-office staff
- Answering customer questions about taxability of items, or sales tax holidays in remote jurisdictions
- Handling audit questions from 46 states
- Paying accountants and computer consultants to answer all these questions

These collection burdens will be a big problem for small catalog and online businesses that collect only their home-state sales tax today. Ask any small business, on Main Street or online, and you'll learn it's hard enough to collect sales tax for one state, let alone all 46 states with sales tax laws of their own.

With that understanding of what small online businesses would face from overturning *Quill*, it's easy to see why House Judiciary Committee members Coble, Griffin, Lundgren, Lofgren, Marino, and Sensenbrenner co--sponsored a resolution to protect our nation's Internet entrepreneurs from new tax collection burdens. H. Res. 95 is titled "Supporting the Preservation of Internet Entrepreneurs and Small Businesses," and its main point is this simple pledge:

Congress should not enact any legislation that would grant State governments the authority to impose *any new burdensome or unfair tax collecting requirements on small online businesses* and entrepreneurs, which would ultimately hurt the economy and consumers in the United States.[18]

The bottom line on "fairness" is that big-box retailers have wielded that term for their own benefit, to the detriment of any small retailers they haven't already extinguished.

HR 3179 IS NOT AN IMPROVEMENT ON QUILL'S PHYSICAL PRESENCE STANDARD

The actual simplification required in HR 3179 is not nearly sufficient to convince Congress that it should abandon its Constitutional role in protecting interstate commerce.

Fortunately, Congress can afford to take the time to design legislation that requires real simplification and makes states accountable to these requirements. As noted above, the uncollected taxes are far lower than tax advocates have claimed: uncollected sales tax on consumer e-commerce is under one percent of all state and local taxes. And the uncollected amounts are not growing as fast as tax advocates have claimed, since the fastest growth in e-commerce is among multi-channel retailers who already collect for states where they have stores –17 of the top 20 e-retailers collect for at least 38 of the 46 sales tax states.[19] And Amazon.com will collect for over half the US population by 2014– under the *Quill* standard of physical presence.

However, if Congress is determined to overturn Constitutional protections for interstate commerce, it must exempt small businesses, require states to adopt minimum simplification requirements, and create fair procedures to resolve sales tax disputes between states and taxpayers. Each of these points are covered below.

HR 3179 DOES NOT INCLUDE ADEQUATE PROTECTION FOR SMALL BUSINESSES

HR 3179 includes a small seller exception that is appropriately mandated by Congress, as opposed to other legislation that leaves it to state tax administrators to set the exception level. But HR 3179 sets the exception threshold at just $1 million in annual remote sales, a number that is far too low for retailers, whose entire expense and payroll must be paid from the margin on sales:

- $1 million in gross sales times 25% average gross margin leaves just $250,000 to cover all costs of running the entire business.
- Those costs include advertising, rent, supplies, insurance, shipping, computers and programming, website, accounting, communications, travel, etc.
- If there's anything left after paying those costs, this business *might* be able to pay an employee or two.

Make no mistake about it - $1 million in retail sales is still just a "mom and pop" operation. The Small Business Administration says a "small" retailer is one with annual sales 20 to 30 times larger than the threshold in HR 3179. The small business tax bill recently passed by the house set a small business threshold at 500 employees, whereas only a few employees could be carried by a retailer with just $1 million in sales.

One way to set a more realistic small seller exception is to exempt all businesses that are out on the "long tail" in terms of e-retail sales. For example, *Internet Retailer* publishes a *Top 500 Guide* each year, ranking the nation's largest retailers on their US e-commerce sales. For 2011, the #1 e-retailer was Amazon.com, at $48 billion in e-retail sales. Number 500 had just $15 million in remote e-retail sales. In total, the Top 500 had $181 billion in e-retail sales.

Economists Eisenach and Litan started with this Top 500 Guide when analyzing where each retailer already collected sales tax under Quill's existing physical presence standard. Using their analysis, we estimated that the Top 500 were responsible for 93% of the uncollected sales tax on US e-commerce in 2011, as shown in the graph below[20] (netchoice.org/top500collect).

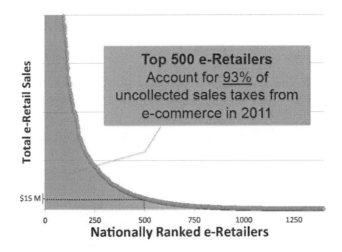

Congress could set a small seller exception that adjusts with inflation and retail trends by exempting sellers below the *Top 500* cutoff from the previous year. Under this method, *the small seller exception for 2012 would have been $15 million in annual sales.* That would leave exempted retailers with a more reasonable gross margin to cover expenses, *while allowing states to recover over 90 percent of the uncollected sales tax on e-retail.*

HR 3179 FAILS TO REQUIRE TRUE TAX SIMPLIFICATION OR REDUCE ADMINISTRATIVE BURDENS

Congress should require robust minimum simplifications before overturning the *Quill* standard of physical presence for states to impose sales tax on remote businesses. Previous Congressional legislation to overturn *Quill* included as many as *16* minimum simplification requirements that SSTP states would have to honor. But HR 3179 requires only *3* measures and they lack essential provisions:

Minimum Simplification Requirements lacking in HR 3179:

- Remote retailers should not be subject to audits from 46 separate state tax authorities. States should respect the outcome of a single audit by any state, on behalf of *all* states.

- Remote retailers should be allowed to use a single sales tax rate for remote sales made into each state, which was the original goal of the SSTP. State lawmakers would, of course, be able to allocate sales tax proceeds among local jurisdictions.
- States should be required to adopt a single set of definitions for taxable and exempt products across *all* states. HR 3179 allows each state to have its own unique definitions:
  "products and services subject to tax must be identical throughout the state"
- States should compensate all businesses for the fair and reasonable cost of collecting sales taxes, taking into account such elements as credit card fees and costs of software implementation and maintenance. Compensation was required in previous federal legislation to overturn the *Quill* physical presence standard, but was dropped in recent versions.
- Remote businesses should not be required to file sales tax returns for all 46 states. All states should accept a single sales tax return filed with a business' home state. The home state revenue department would be responsible for distributing funds to remote states.
- Remote retailers should not be *required* to honor, but may observe, caps and thresholds for sales tax calculation. (an example of a threshold is Massachusetts, where the first $175 of any clothing item is exempt from sales tax[21])
- Remote retailers should not be *required* to honor state-- specific sales tax holidays.
- States should be required to adopt a single rule for sourcing sales. The SSTP originally maintained destination sourcing for all sales tax transactions. But to accommodate origin-based states, SSTP's Governing Board voted to allow origin sourcing for in-state sales while requiring destination sourcing for remote sales. Such "dual sourcing" should not be permitted as part of any federal legislation overturning the physical presence standard.
- States must provide certified software for collection, filing, and remittance. Users of the software would be immune from civil liability for errors in taxes collected. HR 3179 requires software and liability protection only for states that demand remote businesses collect at the local destination rates.

These minimum simplifications should be required for any state that seeks collection authority outside of Quill's physical presence standard, whether as part of HR 3179 or in legislation authorizing collection by SSTP member states.

And if Congress were to grant states taxing powers over out-of-state businesses, it should explicitly prohibit states from otherwise attempting to stretch the definition of physical presence, such as many states have attempted through laws asserting that advertising alone creates nexus.

HR 3179 FAILS TO HOLD STATES ACCOUNTABLE TO SIMPLIFICATION REQUIREMENTS

If Congress grants states the authority to impose sales tax on remote sellers, there must be a mechanism to hold states accountable to the minimum simplification requirements above. HR 3179 subjects states to "a court of competent jurisdiction" to determine whether the state meets minimum requirements. But under the Tax Injunction Act (28 USC §1341), taxpayers are forced to use *state* courts to litigate disputes with state tax collection authorities, even on questions of whether a state is following federal law. It would be far better if federal courts had sole jurisdiction over disputes arising between states and remote businesses regarding a state's compliance with federal law.

CONGRESS COULD CONSIDER A MULTI-STATE COMPACT TO PRESERVE TAX COMPETITION AMONG THE STATES

Congress should retain the benefits of market discipline to restrain states from expanding the complexity of their sales tax systems and skirting the minimum simplification requirements. Fortunately, Congress has a simple way to enforce "tax competition" as part of any legislation that overturns the physical presence standard: *Congress could authorize remote collections through a multi-state compact instead of a national mandate on all businesses.*

HR 3179 would impose collection burdens on businesses in *all 50 states* – including those in states that don't even have a sales tax. Lawmakers in all 50 states would lose the sovereign right to protect their citizens and businesses from tax burdens imposed by other states.

If these new collection burdens are hurting businesses in a state, their legislators won't be able to rescue those businesses if Congress makes collection mandatory for all. This comes as a surprise to many lawmakers who are just beginning to understand the implications of legislation such as HR 3179.

Contrast the national mandate in HR 3179 with a multi-state compact, where states could opt-in if they believed new tax revenues justified having their in-state business collect taxes for other states in the compact. By the same token, states could *opt-out* of the compact if remote state tax burdens were excessive. States opting-out would lose the power to force remote sellers to pay their sales tax, but at least states could protect their own businesses from unreasonable burdens on interstate commerce.

CONCLUSION

Quill's physical presence standard remains a principled and practical way to limit states' imposition of tax burdens on out-of-state businesses. Congress should not sweep *Quill* aside without first requiring that states truly simplify their tax systems and adequately protect small businesses.

End Notes

[1] Steve DelBianco, *Should States Require Online Retailers To Collect Sales Tax?*, Wall Street Journal (Nov. 14, 2011) (emphasis added).

[2] *Nat'l Bellas Hess, Inc. v. Dept. of Rev. of Ill.*, 386 U. S. 753 at 758 (1967).

[3] *Quill Corp. v. North Dakota*, 504 U.S. 298 (1992).

[4] *See Quill Corp. v. North Dakota*, 504 U.S. 298 at 313 FN 6 (1992).

[5] *Id.* at 312 (emphasis added).

[6] Michigan Compiled Laws Of 1979, Chapter 205 Taxation, General Sales Tax Act, § 205.52]

[7] http://www.azdor.gov/business/transactionprivilegetax.aspx

[8] http://www.boe.ca.gov/lawguides/business/current/btlg/vol1/ulsutl/7202.html

[9] "Vertex Press Release (Mar. 21, 2012), available at http://www.vertexinc.com/pressroom/PDF/2012/vertex-address-cleansing.pdf ("At the end of 2011, there were over 9,600 taxing jurisdictions across the U.S. with an average of 651 new and changed sales and use tax rates per year.").

[10] US Census Bureau E-Stats, http://www.census.gov/econ/estats/2010/2010reportfinal.pdf

[11] US Census Bureau E-Stats, http://www2.census.gov/govs/qtax/2011/q2t1.pdf

[12] Eisenach & Litan, *Uncollected Sales Taxes On Electronic Commerce: A Reality Check*, Empiris LLC (Feb. 2010), *available at* http://bit.ly/EisenStudy.

[13] *See* Order of Ct., *The Direct Marketing Ass'n v. Huber* (U.S. Dist. Ct. Colo. Mar. 30, 2012), *and see* 1 Colo. Code Regs. § 201- 1:39-21-112.3.5 (2010).

[14] By 2014 Amazon will collect and remit sales taxes in the following states California, Indiana, Kansas, Kentucky, North Dakota, New York, Pennsylvania, South Carolina, Tennessee, Virginia, and Vermont.

[15] *Quill*, 504 U.S. at 312.

[16] *See* Angus Liten, *Sales-Tax Measures 'to Cost Us Big'*, Wall. St. Jo. (Dec. 1, 2011).

[17] *Available at* http://www.netchoice.org/wp-content/uploads/cost-of-collection-study-sstp.pdf.

[18] H. Res. 95, 112th Cong. (2011) (emphasis added).

[19] Eisenach & Litan, *Uncollected Sales Taxes On Electronic Commerce: A Reality Check*, Empiris LLC (Feb. 2010), *available at* http://bit.ly/EisenStudy.

[20] Top 500 e-Retailers and total e-commerce sales from Internet Retailer, Top 500 Guide, p. 32 (2012 Edition). Top 500 e-retailer tax collection from Eisenach & Litan, Uncollected Sales Taxes On Electronic Commerce: A Reality Check, p.17, 25 (Feb. 2010), available at http://bit.ly/EisenStudy

[21] http://www.mass.gov/dor/individuals/taxpayer-help-and-resources/tax-guides/salesuse-tax-guide.html#apparel

In: Taxation of Internet Sales   ISBN: 978-1-62257-974-7
Editors: Keith Joyner and Carl Sawhill   © 2013 Nova Science Publishers, Inc.

Chapter 13

STATEMENT OF JOSEPH HENCHMAN, VICE PRESIDENT, TAX FOUNDATION. HEARING ON THE "MARKETPLACE EQUITY ACT OF 2011"[*]

The Proper Role of Congress in State Taxation: Ensuring the Interstate Reach of State Taxes Does Not Harm the National Economy

Mr. Chairman, Mr. Ranking Member, and members of the Committee:

I appreciate the opportunity to testify today on Congress's role in the debate over state sales taxation of online purchases. In the 75 years since our founding in 1937, the Tax Foundation has monitored tax policy trends at the federal and state levels, and our data and research is heavily relied upon by policymakers, the media, and the general public. Our analysis is guided by the idea that taxes should be as simple, neutral, transparent, and stable as possible, and as a 501(c)(3) non-profit, non-partisan organization, we take no position on any pending legislation.

---

[*] This is an edited, reformatted and augmented version of the testimony given on July 24, 2012 before the House Judiciary Committee.

We hope that the material we provide will be helpful in the Committee's consideration of the issue.

EXECUTIVE SUMMARY

- After the bitter experience of the Articles of Confederation, the Constitution empowered Congress with the responsibility to rein in state tax overreaching when it threatened to do harm to the national economy.

- Consequently, states were not permitted to tax items in interstate commerce at all, from the Founding until approximately the 1950s.

- Since then, as formally adopted by the U.S. Supreme Court in the *Complete Auto* decision (1977), states may tax interstate commerce so long as the tax is non-discriminatory, fairly apportioned, related to services, and applies only to businesses with substantial presence (nexus).

- In a series of decisions, most recently the *Quill* decision of 1992, the U.S. Supreme Court explained that "substantial nexus" for sales/use tax purposes means physical presence of property or employees. The Court ruled that it exceeds to state powers for them to be able to demand use tax collection from companies that are not physically present in the state.

- States have sought to overrule the *Quill* decision, either legislatively ("Streamlined") or through defiance ("Amazon" tax statutes). The defiance approach in particular has caused significant disruption and uncertainty to the economy.

- Every state with a sales tax also imposes a use tax, levied on taxable items upon which no sales tax has been paid. In other words, use taxes seek to thwart competitive pressure from other states with lower tax rates. Taxpayer compliance with these protectionist use taxes is minimal. (Use tax, with a few exceptions, is imposed on the *consumer* and not the *seller*.)

- Congress has passed a number of statutes limiting the scope of state tax authority on interstate activities ("preemption"), carefully balancing (1) the ability of states to set tax policies in line with their interests and that allow interstate competition for citizens over baskets of taxes and services and (2) limiting state tax power to export tax burdens to non-residents or out-of-state companies, or policies that would excessively harm the free-flow of commerce in the national economy.

- When a resident of a state purchases from a brick-and-mortar retailer, they generally must pay sales tax. When the same resident in the same state purchases the same product from an online retailer, they often do not pay sales tax.
- Many large Internet retailers are expanding the number of states in which they have physical presence, to enable next-day delivery, but that is not the case for many smaller sellers that remain in just one location and use common carriers to deliver purchases.
- There are approximately 9,600 jurisdictions in the United States that collect sales tax, a number that grows by several hundred each year. Subscription tax software is inadequate and can be expensive for occasional sellers, and few states provide adequate tax lookup or consolidated tax filing options. Sales tax can vary by product, by time, and by location in the state. In 7 states, local governments can have a different sales tax base from the state tax base.
- Congress has five basic options on how it may proceed:
  - *Reaffirm the physical presence rule* for sales taxation, and by implication, the disparity of treatment between brick-and-mortar sales and Internet sales.
  - *Reaffirm the physical presence rule* but adopt a new tax approach that mitigates the disparity of treatment between brick-and-mortar sales and Internet sales (such as an origin-based system or a national sales tax on online purchases).
  - *Modify the physical presence rule* in the limited context of state collection of use tax from out-of-state sellers, by those states that have adopted simplified sales tax systems under minimal federal standards, to reduce the harm to interstate commerce. This trade-off would replace the check on state power provided at present by the physical presence rule.
  - *Repeal the physical presence rule* without conditions on the states, granting states unchecked authority to export tax burdens and damage interstate commerce.

- *Do nothing* and risk the continued growth of unchecked and fragmented state authority to export tax burdens and damage interstate commerce.

THE CONSTITUTION EMPOWERS CONGRESS TO LIMIT STATE TAX POWER WHEN IT SEEKS TO SHIFT TAX BURDENS TO NON-RESIDENTS OR DO HARM THE NATIONAL ECONOMY

What you have before you is not a new issue. Absent congressional or judicial checks, states have an incentive to shift tax burdens from physically present individuals and businesses, to those who are beyond their borders. Indeed, it was the states' unchecked behavior in this regard that led to the Constitutional Convention in the first place. Under the Articles of Confederation, states with ports taxed commerce bound for interior states, tariff wars proliferated, and the national economy was imperiled. As Justice Johnson described in 1824, these actions were "destructive to the harmony of the states, and fatal to their commercial interests abroad. This was the immediate cause that led to the forming of a convention."[1]

And so the Constitution was adopted, and through that document, the Congress was granted the power to restrain states from enacting laws that harm the national economy by discriminating against interstate commerce.[2] James Madison noted that these powers would check the "clamors of impatient avidity for immediate and immoderate gain" that drive state legislation discriminating against non-residents.[3] Justice Story later praised the "wisdom and policy in restraining the states themselves from the exercise of [taxation] injuriously to the interests of each other. A petty warfare of regulation is thus prevented, which would rouse resentments, and create dissensions, to the ruin of the harmony and amity of the states."[4]

So strong was this concern that the rule for a century and a half was that states could not tax interstate commerce at all.[5] This eroded in the 1950s and 1960s as it was recognized that those engaged in interstate commerce do enjoy benefits in states where they are present, so it is not unfair to have them support those services with taxes. The complete ban on state taxation of interstate commerce was abandoned in 1977, replaced by a recognition that resident businesses engaged in interstate commerce should pay for the fair share of the state services they consume. In *Complete Auto Transit, Inc. v.*

Brady, the U.S. Supreme Court held that states may tax interstate commerce if the tax meets a four part test:[6]

- **nexus,** *a sufficient connection between the state and the taxpayer;*
- **fair apportionment,** *the state cannot tax beyond its fair share of the taxpayer's income;*
- **nondiscrimination**, *the state must not burden out-of-state taxpayers while exempting in-state taxpayers;*
- **fairly related**, *the tax must be fairly related to services provided to the taxpayer.*

Before and since *Complete Auto*, the courts have routinely exercised this power to restrain state tax infringements on interstate commerce, and these decisions are one of the more non-controversial aspects of constitutional law.[7] Congress has also been active in this area, legislating limits on state tax power where states are incapable of achieving a simplified, uniform system that restrain each state from claiming more than its fair share of taxes on interstate commerce. These have included prohibiting state taxes on food stamps, Federal Reserve banks, interstate airline and bus travel, satellite services, and nonresident members of the military and nonresident members of Congress. Congress has also banned discriminatory state taxes on federal employees, interstate electricity transmission, and interstate railroads (see Table 1).

This power—to limit state tax authority—is not a power to use lightly. There are many components of state tax systems that, frankly, are none of Congress's business, even if they are good or bad public policy. Those aspects of state tax systems that are neither motivated by protectionism nor have the effect of raiding revenue from out-of-staters should be left alone as part of our commitment to fifty simultaneous laboratories for policy experiments, to paraphrase Justice Brandeis.[8] If bad state policy can be corrected by the political pressure of voting resident taxpayers or by the economic pressure of the out-migration of people and dollars, it ought to be left to the states to handle.

However, there are situations where it is vital that Congress use this power, where the alternative is the problem we experienced as a young country under the Articles of Confederation. While everyone is for simple taxes and fair taxes, in practice states look for any advantage or opportunity to shift tax burdens from voting residents to non-voting non-residents, to benefit in-state businesses and individuals by adopting tax policies that discriminate against out-of-state businesses and individuals. For all the discussion about how nonresident companies benefit from state services, the real issue usually is shifting tax burdens away from voting residents to someone else. As Professor Daniel Shaviro has put it, "Perceived tax exportation is a valuable political tool for state legislators, permitting them to claim that they provide government services for free."[9] Without court intervention or congressional action (or the threat of congressional action), efforts to get states to solve interstate tax issues have historically failed, because as soon as a state thinks they can get a bigger share of the pie by breaking the agreement, they do so, and the whole thing unravels.

As one example, the threat of congressional action by the Willis Commission in 1959 led to the adoption of uniform state corporate income tax apportionment rules. This standardization, however, only lasted twenty years before Iowa deviated from it to gain an advantage for itself. Many other states have followed, and today, only 11 states still adhere to the uniform rule. The trend continues to move away from uniformity, not towards it, despite the existence of voluntary organizations like the Multistate Tax Commission (MTC) and the Federation of Tax Administrators (FTA) that exist to advance uniformity in such rules.

NEXUS BASED ON PHYSICAL PRESENCE

We at the Tax Foundation have monitored the increasing use of tax policy by states to do precisely what I have described: shift tax burdens from out-of-state businesses and individuals to benefit in-state businesses and individuals, through discriminatory tax policy. These generally involve disputes over "nexus" standards: the proper scope of state tax power over non-resident individuals and businesses.

Generally, the historical standard is that states may tax those physically present in the jurisdiction, and may not tax those not physically present. This is premised on a view known as the "benefit principle": that the taxes you pay should roughly approximate the services you consume. State spending overwhelmingly, if not completely, is meant to benefit the people who live and work in the jurisdiction. Education, health care, roads, police protection, broadband access, etc.: the primary beneficiaries are state residents. The "benefit principle" thus means that residents should be paying taxes where they work and live, and jurisdictions should not tax those who don't work and live there.

Table 1. Examples of Congressional Preemption of State Tax Authority

4 U.S.C. § 111	Preempting discriminatory state taxation of federal employees
4 U.S.C. § 113	Preempting state taxation of nonresident members of Congress
4 U.S.C. § 114	Preempting discriminatory state taxation of nonresident pensions
7 U.S.C. § 2013	Preempting state taxation of food stamps
12 U.S.C. § 531	Preempting state taxation of Federal Reserve banks, other than real estate taxes
15 U.S.C. § 381 *et seq.*	Preempting state and local income taxes on a business if the business's in-state activity is limited to soliciting sales of tangible personal property, with orders accepted outside the state and goods shipped into the state. (Often referred to as Public L. 86-272.)
15 U.S.C. § 391	Preempting discriminatory state taxes on electricity generation or transmission
31 U.S.C. § 3124	Preempting state taxation of federal debt obligations
43 U.S.C. § 1333 (2)(A)	Preempting state taxation of the outer continental shelf
45 U.S.C. § 101	Preempting state income taxation of nonresident water carrier employees
45 U.S.C. § 501	Preempting state income taxation of nonresident employees of interstate railroads and motor carriers, and Amtrak ticket sales
45 U.S.C. § 801 *et seq.*	Preempting discriminatory state taxation of interstate railroads
47 U.S.C. § 151	Preempting state taxation of Internet access, aside from grandfathered taxes
47 U.S.C. § 152	Preempting local but not state taxation of satellite telecommunications services
49 U.S.C. § 101	Preempting state taxation of interstate bus and motor carrier transportation tickets
49 U.S.C. § 1513 *et seq.*	Preempting state taxation of interstate air carriers and air transportation tickets
49 U.S.C. § 40101	Preempting state income taxation of nonresident airline employees
49 U.S.C. § 40116(b)	Preempting state taxation of air passengers
49 U.S.C. § 40116(c)	Preempting state taxation of flights unless they take off or land in the state
50 U.S.C. § 574	Preempting state taxation of nonresident members of the military stationed temporarily in the state

Source: Tax Foundation compilation.

A physical presence standard for state taxation is in line with this fundamental view of taxation.

Developments have arisen in the three major state tax areas (corporate income tax, individual income tax and sales tax), as well as with some other state taxes (such as telecommunications taxes, taxes on digital goods, car rental taxes, and so forth). Bills have been introduced in the Congress that seek to reaffirm the physical presence rule in these areas (such as BATSA with corporate income tax, Mobile Workforce with individual income tax).

RECENT DEVELOPMENTS IN STATE SALES TAX: OVERVIEW

There are a number of proposals to reverse a series of U.S. Supreme Court decisions (most recently the *Quill* decision of 1992) that prohibit states from imposing sales tax collection obligations on businesses with no property or employee in the state. This "physical presence" standard is meant to prevent states from shifting tax burdens to non-residents away from residents who are the primary beneficiary of state services, while also protecting the free flow of interstate commerce from the compliance costs of non-uniform and numerous (9,600+) sales tax jurisdictions in the United States (see Figure 1, Figure 2, Table 2, and Table 3).

The steadily increasing growth of Internet-based commerce has however led to frustration with this standard, primarily due to disparate sales tax treatment of similar goods within states that has no economic basis. This can be addressed while also ensuring that some standard exists to restrain states from engaging in destructive behavior, such as tax exporting to non-voters or imposing heavy compliance costs on interstate businesses, that the Congress is empowered to prevent. Further, because economic integration is greater now than it has ever been before, the economic costs of nexus uncertainty are also greater today and can ripple through the economy much more quickly.

These actions are only the latest chapter in a long saga over the proper tax treatment of sales made over the Internet, and an even longer saga over the proper scope of state taxing authority. At its core is a dispute over which is more important: limiting state power to tax nonresidents and thus harm the national economy, or ensuring that some transactions do not escape tax because they are conducted online. Discussions following a recent compromise in California, driven by the desire of large Internet retailers to expand their physical presence to enable next-day delivery, suggest that there are policy options that could achieve both ends.

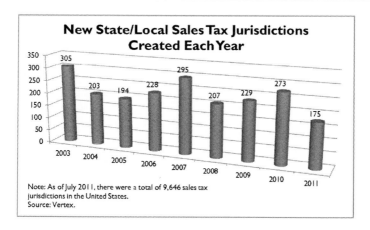

Figure 1. New State/Local Sales Tax Jurisdictions Created Each Year.

Table 2. Example of Sales Tax Complexity: Taxation of a Bottled Frappuccino® Beverage Under Current and Proposed State Legislation

State	Tax on Bottled Frappuccino®?
Enacted	
Arkansas	No
Tennessee	Yes
Virginia	No
West Virginia	Yes
Proposed	
Arizona	No
California	No
Connecticut	Unclear
Hawaii	Yes
Illinois	Yes
Mississippi	Yes
Montana	Yes
New Mexico	Yes
Oregon	No
Rhode Island	No
Tennessee	Yes
Texas	Yes
Utah	Yes
Vermont	Yes

Source: Scott Drenkard, *Overreaching on Obesity: Governments Consider New Taxes on Soda and Candy*, Tax Foundation Special Report No. 196 (Oct. 2011)

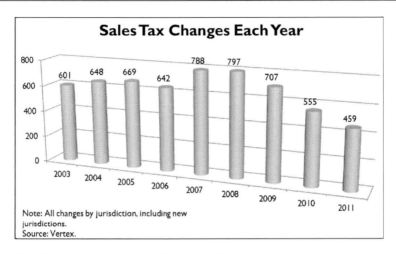

Figure 2. Sales Tax Jurisdictions with Changes Each Year.

Table 3. Other Examples of Contributors to Sales Tax Complexity

States With Local Option Sales Taxes: 37
States That Permit Local Government to Define A Separate Sales Tax Base: **7**
States With Sales Tax Holidays: 17

THE *QUILL* DECISION: NOT A LOOPHOLE, BUT A CHECK ON STATE POWER TO EXPORT TAX BURDENS AND DO HARM INTERSTATE COMMERCE

What is nexus for a remote seller? In 1967, the U.S. Supreme Court held that a business does not have nexus with a state if the business has no retail outlets, solicitors, or property in the state, and communicates with customers only by mail or common carrier as part of a general interstate business.[10] Otherwise, the Court concluded, states could "entangle National's interstate business in a virtual welter of complicated obligations to local jurisdictions with no legitimate claim to impose a fair share of the cost of the local government." This decision was reaffirmed after the *Complete Auto* test was announced in 1977.[11]

During the 1980s, some academics and many states criticized *National Bellas* Hess as archaic, formalistic, and outmoded. Officials were encouraged to ignore the decision, and some state courts disregarded it, even as the number of sales taxes rose from 2,300 to 6,000. Different murky definitions of economic nexus have been proposed:

- Engaged in exploiting the local market on a regular, systematic, large-scale basis.
- Presence of intangible property or affiliates
- Number of customers in state, value of assets or deposits in the state, and receipts attributable to sources in the state
- Analysis of frequency, quantity, and systematic nature of taxpayer's economic contacts with the state
- Derivation of economic benefits from state's residents

Defying the Court rulings, North Dakota enacted a law requiring the out-of-state Quill Corp. to collect sales tax on its sales to 3,000 in-state customers. Any state that advertised three times in the state was liable. In the case, the U.S. Supreme Court reaffirmed *National Bellas Hess* and *Complete Auto*.[12] There they stated that the physical presence rule "firmly establishes the boundaries of legitimate state authority to impose a duty to collect sales and use taxes and reduces litigation concerning those taxes." Justice Byron White dissented, arguing two points that continue to be made today: (1) injustice that some sales escape taxation and (2) arguing that technological change had made discriminatory compliance costs no longer burdensome.

THE STREAMLINED SALES TAX PROJECT HAS WATERED DOWN MEMBERSHIP STANDARDS IN AN UNSUCCESSFUL EFFORT TO ENTICE MORE STATE MEMBERS IN ITS EFFORT TO CHANGE *QUILL*

Today, there are over 9,600 state and local sales tax jurisdictions in the United States. There are different rates on different items, they change frequently, and are not even aligned to 9-digit zip codes. States are reluctant to cooperate on even basic rules and definitions.

The Streamlined Sales Tax Project (SSTP) was launched in 2000 with the mission of getting states to adopt changes to their sales taxes to make them simple and uniform. SSTP then hopes to convince Congress or the courts to overrule *Quill* and allow use tax collection obligations on out-of-state companies ("Main Street Fairness Act").

However, the SSTP has abandoned simplification efforts and any attempt to reduce the number of sales tax jurisdictions, instead focusing on uniformity efforts. In many cases, the Project has enabled state sales tax complexity by permitting separate tax rates for certain goods. States generally are reluctant to yield parochial advantages, even with the possibility of online sales tax revenue in return, undermining their argument to Congress as part of the Main Street Fairness Act that they have succeeded in their mission. Large states have generally avoided the SSTP, and membership has been stuck at ~20 states for some time. This in turn has led to impatience from states and others.

SOME STATES HAVE SOUGHT TO DEFY *QUILL* THROUGH UNCONSTITUTIONAL LEGISLATION

In 2008, New York adopted an "Amazon" tax, nicknamed after the Internet retailer as the most visible target. The law held that a person or business with no physical presence in the state nevertheless has nexus if it (1) enters into agreement with in-state resident involving commissions for referring potential customers; and (2) has gross receipts from sales by out-of-state company from referrals within the state are more than $10,000 in a 12-month period.

Amazon.com & Overstock.com responded by terminating affiliate programs in New York, and Amazon.com filed a lawsuit in state court. The law was upheld by a trial judge (New York's trial courts are called the "New York Supreme Court," causing confusion about who upheld the Amazon tax as constitutional); the judge concluded that Amazon.com's in-state affiliates are necessary and significant to establishing and maintaining out-of-state company's market in the state. But because they make up only 1.5% of sales, that was the basis for the appeal. The New York Supreme Court, Appellate Division ruled in late 2010 that law is not facially unconstitutional but may be unconstitutional for Amazon. The case was remanded to the lower court, but Amazon is appealing to state's highest court, the New York Court of Appeals. The case is ongoing.

In 2009, Rhode Island and North Carolina adopted identical New York-style laws. Neither has seen any revenue and Rhode Island has actually seen revenue loss due to reduced income tax collections from terminated in-state affiliates. Laws were also passed in California and Hawaii but vetoed. (See Table 4 for a status of all state efforts to defy *Quill* legislatively.)

In 2010, Colorado considered the same law but faced opposition from in-state affiliates. Instead it adopted a law (H.B. 10-1193) designed to push Amazon into collecting use taxes without explicitly requiring it. Any out-of-state retailer that is part of "a controlled group of corporations" with at least one member with physical presence in Colorado, all the retailers in the group have nexus with Colorado. However, the "only" obligation with this nexus is notification:

- "[N]otify Colorado purchasers that sales or use tax is due on certain purchases made from the retailer and that the State of Colorado requires the purchaser to file a sales or use tax return." Penalty of $5 per failure per customer, plus criminal penalties.
- "[Notify] all Colorado purchasers by January 31 of each year showing such information as the Colorado Department of Revenue shall require by rule and the total amount paid by the purchaser for Colorado purchases made from the retailer in the previous calendar year. Such notification shall include, if available, the dates of purchases, the amounts of each purchase, and the category of the purchase, including, if known by the retailer, whether the purchase is exempt or not exempt from taxation." Must be sent separately from shipments and be by first-class mail. CC to State. Penalty of $10 per failure per customer, plus criminal penalties.

Amazon.com terminated affiliate programs in Colorado. In January 2010, a federal judge stayed the law stayed as probably unconstitutional on First Amendment grounds, and the law was thrown out completely in April 2012.[13]

North Carolina followed Colorado by adopting regulation with similar/notification requirements. They demanded out-of-state companies provide them with all customer purchase information dating from 2003, by April 19, 2010. Amazon.com and the ACLU filed lawsuit in federal court, arguing that "[e]ach order of a book, movie, CD or other expressive work potentially reveals an intimate fact about an Amazon customer" (see Table 5).

A federal judge struck down the North Carolina regulation as violating First Amendment in October 2010. In 2011, Illinois and Arkansas enacted New York-style laws (the Illinois law was subsequently ruled unconstitutional). California enacted one but after a possible repeal referendum was proposed, the state and Amazon.com reached an agreement whereby Amazon.com will develop a physical presence in the state (i.e., build warehouses).

Table 4. Status of State Efforts to Defy *Quill* Legislatively

Arkansas	Enacted mid-2011.
California	Enacted mid-2011 but effective date postponed after agreement reached with state.
Colorado	Enacted 2010. Ruled unconstitutional.
Connecticut	Enacted mid-2011.
Illinois	Enacted 2011. Ruled unconstitutional.
New York	Enacted 2008. In litigation.
North Carolina	Enacted 2009. Ruled unconstitutional.
Rhode Island	Enacted 2009. Officials report that the law has reduced state tax collections. May be repealed.

Source: Tax Foundation compilation. Does not include states where legislation was proposed but not adopted.

Table 5. Examples of Purchases Required to Be Disclosed to State Officials under the North Carolina Law

Bipolar Disorder: A Guide for Parents and Families
He Had It Coming: How to Outsmart Your Husband and Win Your Divorce
Living with Alcoholism: Your Guide to Dealing with Alcohol Abuse and Addiction While Getting the Alcoholism Treatment You Need
What to Do When You Can't Get Pregnant: The Complete Guide to All the Technologies for Couples Facing Fertility Problems
Outing Yourself: How to Come out as Lesbian or Gay to Your Family, Friends, and Coworkers
Lolita (1962)
Brokeback Mountain (2005)
Fahrenheit 9/11 (2004)

Source: ACLU brief in the North Carolina case.

While for the most part unsuccessful, these state efforts have highlighted the desire to modify the *Quill* holding in some way. This pressure is likely to continue.

POSSIBLE SOLUTIONS

Substantial progress has been made in recent months toward possible solutions that could (1) simplify sales tax systems and avoid discriminatory compliance costs, (2) eliminate non-neutral tax rates on similar products sold by online and brick-and-mortar businesses, (3) limit taxation in a state to those residents who enjoy the benefits of state services, (4) prevent multiple taxation of interstate commerce, and (5) prevent unconstitutional and fragmented state attempts to impose such tax burdens in a destructive manner.

Congress has five basic options on how it may proceed:

- *Reaffirm the physical presence rule* for sales taxation, and by implication, the disparity of treatment between brick-and-mortar sales and Internet sales.
- *Reaffirm the physical presence rule* but adopt a new tax approach that mitigates the disparity of treatment between brick-and-mortar sales and Internet sales (such as an origin-based system or a national sales tax on online purchases).
- *Modify the physical presence rule* in the limited context of state collection of use tax from out-of-state sellers, by those states that have adopted simplified sales tax systems under minimal federal standards, to reduce the harm to interstate commerce. This trade-off would replace the check on state power provided at present by the physical presence rule.
- *Repeal the physical presence rule* without conditions on the states, granting states unchecked authority to export tax burdens and damage interstate commerce.
- *Do nothing* and risk the continued growth of unchecked and fragmented state authority to export tax burdens and damage interstate commerce.

I'll focus the remainder of my analysis on the third option, which would allow the states to collect use tax from remote sellers on condition that they simplify their sales tax systems in accordance with minimum federal specifications. If the Committee is interested in further discussion of the other alternatives, we will be happy to do so.

The Marketplace Equity Act (H.R. 3179) and Marketplace Fairness Act (S. 1832) are two recent proposals that would eliminate the physical presence rule but otherwise make advances towards ensuring that states reduce the burdens associated with collecting their sales taxes. Example provisions include requirements that states have a single state-level agency that administer all sales tax rules, offer one tax return and audit for the entire state, require one uniform tax base for the entire state, provide software that identifies the applicable tax rate for a sale, including local rates and hold sellers harmless for any software errors or mistakes by the state, provide 30 days' notice of any local sales tax rate change, and exempt sellers with a *de minimis* level of collections. (See Table 6 for a comparison.)

Effective simplification is a necessity for any federal proposal.

Table 6. Provisions of Current Pending Federal Legislation

Before Collecting Remote Use Tax, State Must...	Marketplace Equity Act	Marketplace Fairness Act	Main Street Fairness Act
Designate one state entity to collect, process, and audit returns for all tax jurisdictions in the state.	✓	✓	✓
Establish unified audit of remote sellers for all taxing jurisdictions in the state.	✗	✓	✗
Establish a single tax return for all taxing jurisdictions in the state.	✓	✓	✓
Provide or certify tax collection and remittance software. (Note: Not necessarily free software)	✓	✓	✓
Hold remote sellers harmless for errors in state-provided software.	✓	✓	✓
Adopt standardized definitions of commonly taxed goods.	✗	✗	✓
Offer immunity to remote sellers who misapply sales tax holidays.	✗	✗	✗
Compensate vendors.	✗	✗	✓
Offer a single statewide blended rate as an option.	✓	✗	✗
Require local jurisdictions to use the state's sales tax base.	✓	✓	✓
Require local jurisdictions to align geographically with 5-digit zip codes	✗	✗	✗
Legislation explicitly preempts other state efforts to force use tax collection by tax out-of-state sellers.	✗	✗	✗
"Small seller exception"	$1m in U.S., $100k in state	$500k in U.S.	To be set
Legislation establishes federal court jurisdiction for enforcing simplification standards.	✗	✗	✓

Source: Tax Foundation review of legislation. Main Street Fairness Act review includes only provisions incorporated in federal law, not those merely adopted by its Governing Board.

All these simplifications are desirable, and together would provide a sufficient check on state tax overreaching while leaving ample space for states to structure their tax systems and rates in line with their own preferences. The only infringement on state sovereignty is an infringement on state power to burden interstate commerce with problematic tax policy.

Sales Tax: Combined State and Average Local Rates
Tax Year 2012

Note: Some states levy gross receipts taxes in addition to sales taxes. See Table 20 for information on gross receipts taxes.

(a) City, county and municipal rates vary. These rates are weighted by population to compute an average local tax rate. (b) Three states collect a separate, uniform "local" add-on sales tax: California (1%), Utah (1.25%), Virginia (1%). We include these in their state sales tax. (c) The sales taxes in Hawaii, New Mexico and South Dakota have broad bases that include many services, so their rates are not strictly comparable to other states. (d) Due to data limitations, table does not include sales taxes in local resort areas in Montana. (e) Some counties in New Jersey are not subject to the statewide sales tax rate and collect a local rate of 3.5%. Their average local score is represented as a negative.

Source: Tax Foundation; Sales Tax Clearinghouse.

Congress has passed a number of statutes limiting the scope of state tax authority on interstate activities, carefully balancing (1) the ability of states to set tax policies in line with their interests and that allow interstate competition for citizens over baskets of taxes and services and (2) limiting state tax power to export tax burdens to non-residents or out-of-state companies, or policies that would excessively harm the free-flow of commerce in the national economy. A package specifying a floor of all the simplifications listed in Table 6 would be welcome and would greatly reduce constraints on economic growth.

State and Local Sales Tax Rates As of January 1, 2012

State	State Tax Rate	Rank	Avg. Local Tax Rate (a)	Combined Rate	Rank
Ala.	4.00%	38	4.33%	8.33%	8
Alaska	None	46	1.77%	1.77%	46
Ariz.	6.60%	9	2.52%	9.12%	2
Ark.	6.00%	16	2.58%	8.58%	6
Calif. (b)	7.25%	1	0.86%	8.11%	12
Colo.	2.90%	45	4.54%	7.44%	15
Conn.	6.35%	11	None	6.35%	31
Del.	None	46	None	0.00%	47
Fla.	6.00%	16	0.62%	6.62%	29
Ga.	4.00%	38	2.84%	6.84%	24
Hawaii (c)	4.00%	38	0.35%	4.35%	45
Idaho	6.00%	16	0.02%	6.02%	35
Ill.	6.25%	13	1.95%	8.20%	10
Ind.	7.00%	2	None	7.00%	20
Iowa	6.00%	16	0.81%	6.81%	25
Kans.	6.30%	12	1.96%	8.26%	9
Ky.	6.00%	16	None	6.00%	36
La.	4.00%	38	4.85%	8.85%	3
Maine	5.00%	31	None	5.00%	43
Md.	6.00%	16	None	6.00%	36
Mass.	6.25%	13	None	6.25%	33
Mich.	6.00%	16	None	6.00%	36
Minn.	6.875%	7	0.30%	7.18%	17
Miss.	7.00%	2	0.004%	7.00%	19
Mo.	4.225%	37	3.26%	7.49%	14
Mont. (d)	None	46	None	0.00%	47

State	State Tax Rate	Rank	Avg. Local Tax Rate (a)	Combined Rate	Rank
Nebr.	5.50%	28	1.27%	6.77%	26
Nev.	6.85%	8	1.08%	7.93%	13
N.H.	None	46	None	0.00%	47
N.J. (e)	7.00%	2	-0.03%	6.97%	22
N.M. (c)	5.125%	30	2.12%	7.24%	16
N.Y.	4.00%	38	4.48%	8.48%	7
N.C.	4.75%	35	2.10%	6.85%	23
N.D.	5.00%	31	1.39%	6.39%	30
Ohio	5.50%	28	1.25%	6.75%	27
Okla.	4.50%	36	4.16%	8.66%	5
Ore.	None	46	None	0.00%	47
Pa.	6.00%	16	0.34%	6.34%	32
R.I.	7.00%	2	None	7.00%	20
S.C.	6.00%	16	1.13%	7.13%	18
S.D.	4.00%	38	1.39%	5.39%	41
Tenn.	7.00%	2	2.45%	9.45%	1
Tex.	6.25%	13	1.89%	8.14%	11
Utah (b)	5.95%	27	0.73%	6.68%	28
Vt.	6.00%	16	0.14%	6.14%	34
Va. (b)	5.00%	31	None	5.00%	43
Wash.	6.50%	10	2.30%	8.80%	4
W.Va.	6.00%	16	None	6.00%	36
Wis.	5.00%	31	0.43%	5.43%	40
Wyo.	4.00%	38	1.34%	5.34%	42
D.C.	6.00%	(16)	-	6.00%	(36)

CONCLUSION

Businesses throughout our nation's history have plied their trade across state lines. Today, with new technologies, even the smallest businesses can sell their products and services in all fifty states through the Internet and through the mail. Business travel is easier than ever before. If such sales, travel, or activity can now expose these businesses to tax compliance and liability risks in states where they merely have customers, they will be less likely to expand their reach into those states. Interstate commerce is not a golden goose that can be squeezed without adverse effects on economic growth. Unless a single uniform nexus standard is established, the conflicting standards will impede the desire and the ability of businesses to expand, which harms the nation's economic growth potential.

We at the Tax Foundation track the numerous rates, bases, exemptions, credits, adjustments, phaseouts, exclusions, and deductions that litter our federal and state tax codes. Frequent and ambiguous alterations of tax codes and the confusion they cause are a key source of the growing tax compliance burden. We have several staffers as well as computer-based and publication subscriptions dedicated to being up to date and accurate on the frequent changes to the many taxes in our country, but even we have trouble doing it. It would be extremely difficult for individuals and businesses who are in business to sell a good or service, not to conduct tax policy research.

Congress can obtain evidence from interested stakeholders and take political and economic factors into consideration when developing new rules of taxation. The Supreme Court, by contrast, must develop broad doctrine in a case-by-case fashion, based on the facts of the particular case before them. (Additionally, the Court seems to have an aversion to tax cases in general and these type of tax cases in particular.) This is why congressional action, which can be more comprehensive and accountable than judicial action, and can better address issues of transition, retroactivity, and *de minimis* exemptions, may now be the best vehicle for preventing burdens to interstate commerce. It is up to Congress to exercise its power to protect interstate commerce.

We now live in a world of iPods, telecommuting, and Amazon.com. It is a testament to the Framers that their warnings about states' incentives to hinder the national economy remain true today.

Some may argue that faster roads and powerful computers mean that states should now be able to tax everything everywhere. While some constitutional principles surely must be revisited to be applied to new circumstances, the idea that parochial state interests should not be permitted to burden interstate commerce remains a timeless principle regardless of how sophisticated technology may become.

End Notes

[1] *See, e.g., Gibbons v. Ogden*, 22 U.S. (9 Wheat.) 1, 224 (1824) (Johnson, J., concurring).

[2] *See* U.S. CONST. art. I, §8, cl. 3 (Interstate Commerce Clause); U.S. CONST. art. I, §10, cl. 2 (Import-Export Clause); U.S. CONST. art. I, §10, cl. 3 (Tonnage Clause); U.S. CONST. art. IV, § 2, cl. 1 (Privileges and Immunities Clause); U.S. CONST., amend. XIV, §1 (Privileges or Immunities Clause).

[3] James Madison, THE FEDERALIST NO. 42 (1788).

[4] 1 STORY CONST § 497.

[5] *See, e.g., Freeman v. Hewit*, 329 U.S. 249, 252-53 (1946) ("A State is ... precluded from taking any action which may fairly be deemed to have the effect of impeding the free flow of trade between States"); *Leloup v. Port of Mobile*, 127 U.S. 640, 648 (1888) ("No State has the right to lay a tax on interstate commerce in any form.").

[6] 430 U.S. 274 (1977).

[7] The power of the federal courts to act when Congress is silent is inferred as an implication of the Commerce Clause, a doctrine often referred to as the "dormant" or "negative" Commerce Clause. *See, e.g., Willson v. The Black Bird Creek Marsh Co.*, 27 U.S. 245 (1829). The Commerce Clause prohibits states from imposing a tax on activity out-of-state while leaving identical activity in-state untaxed. *See Boston Stock Exchange v. State Tax Comm'n*, 429 U.S. 318 (1977) (invalidating a New York tax imposed solely on activity out-of-state while leaving identical activity in-state untaxed); *Westinghouse Elec. Co. v. Tully*, 466 U.S. 388 (1984) (invalidating a New York scheme exempting activity in-state while simultaneously imposed a tax on identical activity out-of-state); *Bacchus Imports, Ltd. v. Dias*, 468 U.S. 263 (1984) (invalidating a Hawaii tax imposed on a category of products but exempting activity in-state); *Am. Trucking Ass'n v. Scheiner*, 483 U.S. 266 (1987) (invalidating a Pennsylvania scheme imposing fees on all trucks while reducing other taxes for trucks in-state only); *New Energy Co. v. Limbach*, 486 U.S. 269 (1988) (invalidating an Ohio tax credit to all ethanol producers but disallowed for non-Ohio producers); *West Lynn Creamery, Inc. v. Healy*, 512 U.S. 186 (1994) (invalidating a Massachusetts general tax on dairy producers where the revenue was then distributed to domestic dairy producers); *Camps/Newfound/Owatanna, Inc. v. Town of Harrison*, 520 U.S. 564 (1997) (invalidating Maine's denial of the general charitable deduction to organizations that primarily serve non-

Maine residents). *But see Dep't. of Revenue of Ky. v. Davis*, 553 U.S. 328 (2008) (upholding Kentucky's exclusion from tax of interest earned from its state bonds, but not other states bonds, on the grounds that Kentucky is acting as a market participant no different from any other bond issuer).

The Import-Export Clause prohibits states from penalizing activity that crosses state lines, particularly imports. *See, e.g., Michelin Corp. v. Wages*, 423 U.S. 276, 295 (1976) (stating that the Import-Export Clause prohibits import taxes that "create special protective tariffs or particular preferences for certain domestic goods...."). Justice Clarence Thomas, a critic of dormant commerce clause jurisprudence, nonetheless argues that taxes that discriminate against nonresidents should be invalidated by the courts under the Import-Export Clause. *See Camps/Newfound/Owatanna*, 520 U.S. at 610 (Thomas, J., dissenting) ("That the expansion effected by today's decision finds some support in the morass of our negative Commerce Clause case law only serves to highlight the need to abandon that failed jurisprudence and to consider restoring the original Import-Export Clause check on discriminatory state taxation to what appears to be its proper role.").

The Tonnage Clause prohibits charges on shipping freight.

The Privileges and Immunities Clause of Article IV and the Privileges or Immunities Clause of the Fourteenth Amendment protects the right of citizens to cross state lines in pursuit of an honest living. *See, e.g., United Bldg. & Constr. Trades v. Mayor*, 465 U.S. 208, 219 (1984) (identifying "pursuit of a common calling" as a privilege of citizenship protected by the Constitution); *Saenz v. Roe*, 526 U.S. 489 (1999) (invalidating a law that did not restrict state travel *per se* but discouraged the crossing of state lines with a punitive and discriminatory law); *id.* at 511 (Rehnquist, J., dissenting) ("The right to travel clearly embraces the right to go from one place to another, and prohibits States from impeding the free passage of citizens); Erwin Chemerinsky, CONSTITUTIONAL LAW 450 (2d ed. 2002) ("The vast majority of cases under the [Article IV] privileges and immunities clause involve states discriminating against out-of-staters with regard to their ability to earn a livelihood.").

[8] *See New State Ice Co. v. Liebmann*, 285 U.S. 262, 311 (1932) (Brandeis, J., dissenting) ("It is one of the happy incidents of the federal system that a single courageous State may, if its citizens choose, serve as a laboratory; and try novel social and economic experiments without risk to the rest of the country.").

[9] Daniel Shaviro, "An Economic and Political Look at Federalism in Taxation," 90 Mich. L. Rev. 895, 957 (1992).

[10] *See National Bellas Hess, Inc. v. Dept. of Revenue of Ill.*, 386 U.S. 753, 759-60 (1967).

[11] *See Nat'l Geographic Society v. Ca. Bd. Of Equalization*, 430 U.S. 551, 559 (1977).

[12] *See Quill Corp. v. North Dakota*, 504 U.S. 298 (1992).

[13] *See* Mark Robyn, "Colorado Amazon Regulations Ruled Unconstitutional," (Apr. 4, 2012), http://www.taxfoundation.org/blog/show/28111.html

INDEX

D

E